INSURGENT TRUTH

INSURGENT TRUTH

*Chelsea Manning and the Politics
of Outsider Truth-Telling*

LIDA MAXWELL

OXFORD
UNIVERSITY PRESS

OXFORD
UNIVERSITY PRESS

Oxford University Press is a department of the University of Oxford. It furthers
the University's objective of excellence in research, scholarship, and education
by publishing worldwide. Oxford is a registered trade mark of Oxford University
Press in the UK and certain other countries.

Published in the United States of America by Oxford University Press
198 Madison Avenue, New York, NY 10016, United States of America.

© Oxford University Press 2019

CIP data is on file at the Library of Congress
ISBN 978-0-19-092003-6 (pbk.)
ISBN 978-0-19-092002-9 (hbk.)

9 8 7 6 5 4 3 2 1

Paperback printed by Webcom, Inc., Canada
Hardback printed by Bridgeport National Bindery, Inc., United States of America

For Japonica

CONTENTS

PREFACE: CASSANDRA AND
SOCRATES

What does a truth-teller look like? An image of a man immediately leaps into view. It is a man who puts aside his own economic and social interests in favor of the truth and who sees
his devotion to truth as serving his city or country. It is a man
who believes he can tell the truth only by living truthfully,
who is willing to sacrifice his life and well-being on behalf of
truth. In the twentieth and twenty-first centuries, many citizens, writers, and thinkers have called this man Socrates. In
the writings of Martin Luther King Jr., Henry David Thoreau,
and Mohandas Gandhi, Socrates appears as a heroic figure,
whose commitment to the truth in the face of injustice stands
as a model for contemporary gadflies advocating on behalf
of racial or anti-colonial justice.[1] In the writings of Hannah
Arendt, Michel Foucault, and others, Socrates's example
appears similarly heroic and virtuosic: an example of an individual willing to sacrifice himself in ways large and small

on behalf of the truthfulness of himself and his city.[2] In these narratives of Socrates's life and death, his words and actions compose a monument to his practice and conception of philosophical truth-telling: the pursuit of non-contradiction.[3]

Yet if Socrates inhabits the heroic foreground of our truth-telling imaginary, there is another image that persists alongside it, even if its contours are more difficult to ascertain, its features slightly out of focus. In post-Homeric mythology, Cassandra appears as a visionary who knew and proclaimed the truth of the destruction to come for Troy and for herself during the Trojan War, but was not believed by her fellow Trojans. A daughter of King Priam sent to be a priestess in Apollo's temple, Cassandra refused Apollo's demand for sex and was cursed to know the truth but never be believed: "He [Apollo] came like a wrestler,/magnificent, took me down and breathed his fire/through me and— . . . I yielded, then at the climax I recoiled—I deceived Apollo!/ . . . Even then I told my people all the grief to come . . . /Once I betrayed him I could never be believed."[4] In speaking to the Trojan people, Cassandra proclaimed the earthly truth of the Trojan War: it was to bring destruction, slavery, and death to her people and city. Cassandra did not see the truth because she had chosen (as Socrates did) to live as a philosopher; rather, she saw the destructive force of violence and war because she was vulnerable to those violences herself. Cassandra's truth-telling was thus not (as it was for Socrates) a practice of risking her private interests on behalf of the public good; rather, she told the truth from a position of public and private marginalization, where everything had already been risked. Yet as a woman who refused to acquiesce to male and divine sexual desire, Cassandra was cursed to never look like a truth teller; rather, she appeared untrustworthy, suspect, mad.

In some respects, Socrates and Cassandra appear similar characters. Both truth-tellers in times of war and unrest, both feared by some parts of their society, both rendered outcasts, they told the truth and were not believed. They both also ultimately lost their lives because of the social disturbance they and their truth-telling caused. Yet I have begun by drawing out differences between their examples because I am interested in asking how our understanding of truth-telling in politics might shift if we took Cassandra rather than Socrates as our archetypical truth-teller. Invoked as a model for what we now call civil disobedience, Socrates appears as an exemplar of seeking absolute truth and justice over and above unjust, biased state and local laws and edicts.[5] Through reference to his example, political theorists have been able to raise important questions about truth-tellers (philosophers, activists, experts, movement leaders) confronting an intransigent demos—that is, questions about why a people whose passions, or love of sophistry, or desire for wealth makes them unable to recognize truth.

Yet Socrates's example does not raise—or raises less obviously than Cassandra's—the question of how someone appears legible as a truth-teller in the first place. Put differently, Socrates's example tends to suggest that conflicts over truth in politics are due either to popular passions or ignorance of truth,[6] rather than asking how various forms of power function to keep different kinds of individuals (women, people of color, queer, trans*, and gender nonconforming people) outside the circle of the hearable. Hierarchies of citizenship, class, and gender set the boundaries of Socrates's political conflict about truth with his fellow Athenians; figures like Cassandra were always already illegible, and their reality appears always already insignificant to their society.

If Socrates's predicament helps to illuminate the pre-dicament of Thoreau and Gandhi, Cassandra's predicament gestures toward a different set of experiences: of ordinary women who tell the truth about sexual assault, and are not believed;[7] of people of color who tell the truth about police violence, brutality, and killing and are not believed; of queer, trans*, and gender nonconforming people who tell the truth about violence, bullying, and the social invisibility of wrongs done to them, and are not believed; of those trying to tell the truth about war's violence and oppression, and are not believed; and of others, excluded from the circle of the hear-able, who are trying to create a meaningful place in the world by telling the truth about their exclusion from it.[8] Cassandra's predicament is not the predicament of heroes and great men; rather, her predicament helps attune us to the significance of experiences of women, trans* people, queers, and people of color trying to tell the truth so that they might survive, de-mand a society in which their reality matters, and create the possibility of living differently.[9]

To be clear, Cassandra and contemporary marginalized individuals are not cast as suspect, un-believable, and mad *only* because of their identity. Rather, they also tell truths that are unsettling to power and privilege. In different ways, they offer their societies what I call *insurgent truth*: a kind of truth that does not stabilize society by offering prepolitical facts but instead unsettles society by showing that the so-cial ground is already rough, exclusive, and often lop-sided. Cassandra told the Trojans that they would lose the war and be totally destroyed. Black Lives Matter activists tell Americans that their society is premised on White su-premacy and the presumed worthlessness of Black lives.[10] Women in the #MeToo movement tell their fellow citizens that their governments and workplaces are saturated and constituted by misogyny and sexual harassment. In other words, if Cassandra and contemporary marginalized truth-tellers are cast as suspect in part because of who they are, they are also portrayed as un-believable because of the truths they tell. This is no accident: the sustenance of political and social hierarchies in an ostensibly just society depends on portraying the marginalized as unreliable observers of their own marginalization and portraying the oppressed as un-trustworthy witnesses to their own oppression.

If we focus our attention on the hierarchies of credibility and truth foregrounded by Cassandra's example, then the question with which I began, "What does a truth-teller look like?," no longer seems appropriate. This question suggests that social credibility is inextricably linked to a certain identity or self-presentation, whereas Cassandra's example suggests that social norms, institutions, violence, and ideology *produce* certain identities and comportments as more credible. If social credibility is a product of social and political organization, then it seems better to put the question this way: "How does the institutional, legal, affective, and discursive *staging of political scenes* make some people look like truth-tellers, and others not?"

While the rest of this book will not focus on Cassandra, I open with her example because it offers an alternative, critical horizon of possibility in which to examine the significance of the different kinds of truth-telling that Cassandra and contemporary marginalized individuals enact. For the remainder of the book, I will call these forms of truth-telling—where individuals illegible to their societies *as* truth-tellers tell insurgent truths—"outsider truth-telling." Contrasting outsider truth-telling with Socrates's example may seem to set him up (along with the Western philosophical tradition that he inaugurated) as representatives of "insiders," hierarchy, and the dominant class. Indeed, almost everyone who read drafts of this book worried that I did not render Socrates a complex enough figure and that I did not underline sufficiently that he, too, was an outsider. If I have given short shrift to Socrates here, it is not because I think he is not complex, interesting, and important. Indeed, many people have written excellent books about Socrates's truth-telling, his example for democratic politics, and his critical sensibility (among other things)—and I have been compelled by many of them.[11] Yet the very depth and size of this body of work on Socrates testifies, in my view, to the need to expend some energy on those examples of truth-telling that may be obscured by focusing on someone who was, after all, a male citizen and member of the Athenian elite, even though his fellow elites eventually turned on him. If his example offers a recognizable model for telling unpopular truths, I want to ask: What forms of truth-telling may appear *unrecognizable* in terms of Socrates's example? I am thus less interested in doing full justice to Socrates's example in this preface (there are many books that pursue this project) and instead more interested in asking another question: What forms of truth-telling become more fully legible, and what kinds of worlds appear more fully illuminated, by thinking through the example of Cassandra and others who tell unsettling truths, even when their societies tell them they are incapable of telling the truth?

The primary contemporary example of Cassandra's predicament that I engage in this book is Chelsea Manning's leaking of government documents. Like Cassandra, Manning told the truth about war and a social order sustained by it. Her truth-telling, also like Cassandra's, revealed her illegibility in both public and private realms: in both, she, as a gender nonconforming individual, appeared an improper truth-teller. And Manning's truth-telling, like Cassandra's, unsettled hierarchies of truth-telling that prop up a discriminatory and often oppressive social order. I read Manning not as an isolated political actor, but instead as an outsider truth-teller within a cohort of outsider truth-tellers (such as Virginia Woolf, Bayard Rustin, Audre Lorde), whose practices are distinct yet connected, and whose significance becomes more apparent when read in conjunction with each other.

In her novelistic re-telling of Cassandra's story,[12] the German writer Christa Wolf portrays Cassandra's truth-telling not as the result of a divine curse but instead as a capacity nurtured by Cassandra's enmeshment in what Virginia Woolf would call an "Outsiders' Society": a group of female outcasts (slaves, Amazons, midwives, some "elite" women like Cassandra) who gather in a cave outside the bounds of the city of Troy. Through practices of story-telling, ritual, and practically sustaining a way of life outside the strictures of war, these women create an atmosphere where, in contrast to Trojan men's bewitchment into the mythology of war, Cassandra is able to see reality: the oppression of women, generated and sustained in large part by her brothers' and father's commitment to a violent, endless war that results in their death. In Wolf's novel, the outsider capacity for truth-telling is thus nurtured not through the abstract dialectic and interrogation favored by Socrates, but rather through staging a new political scene, and creating a new outsider space, that refuses the terms of the war society. Through co-existing with other outsiders in a space that is not organized by war and status-seeking, Cassandra learns to trust and speak her own perceptions of reality.

If literally leaving the bounds of the war society and helping to create (even if only fleetingly) a space outside war was an option for Cassandra, that seems an impossibility now. Yet might outsider spaces and solidarities—that exceed and resist the terms of public and private—still come into being, even in the midst of technology, military and prison systems, and economic imperatives that interpolate us all into war societies? My argument, which will unfold in the following chapters, is that they are already there. From Manning's internet chats and prison friendships, to Woolf's outsiders standing on bridges and telling unsettling truths in dining rooms, to Anna Julia Cooper whispering truth from a "coigne of vantage" in the public realm, to Rustin's persistent queerness in Left, pacifist spaces in the 1940s and 1950s, I will suggest that outsider truth-tellers change spaces by telling or enacting the truth with others and that their truth-telling depends on collectively transformed spaces.

In a time when the value and meaning of truth-telling and politics is very much up for debate, *Insurgent Truth* develops a defense of the value of outsider truth-telling as a practice that generates reality, facts, and evidence about our world *not* to sustain a prepolitical common ground but instead on behalf of *unsettling* a supposedly common ground and creating, through its practice, new models of what it means to live collectively, stably, and truthfully.

CHELSEA MANNING

AND THE POLITICS

OF TRUTH-TELLING

IN MAY 2010, CHELSEA MANNING[1] was arrested for allegedly leaking troves of US top-secret information to Wikileaks.[2] The leaked information came to be known as the Iraq war logs, the Afghan war logs, and Cablegate. Manning also leaked raw video and audio footage of US soldiers in a helicopter shooting down an unarmed Reuters employee, along with others—footage that Julian Assange of Wikileaks edited and released in more polished form as *Collateral Murder*. In contrast to Edward Snowden's leaking of National Security Agency documents, which happened two years later, Manning was not primarily interested in revealing governmental intrusions on privacy. Rather, Manning's focus was on US abuses abroad: unreported killing of civilians; the failure to adequately investigate accusations of torture; increased use of drones; and the use of special units to track down and kill individuals without trial, among other things. Manning's leaks, in other words, were anti-war leaks.

Manning also believed that the diplomatic cables she leaked revealed how the "first world oppressed the third."[3]

In an early profile of Manning in the *New York Times* that presaged broader media coverage, Ginger Thompson suggested that Manning leaked the documents out of "private" interests—out of revenge for being bullied in the military or for her struggles under Don't Ask Don't Tell, or out of "delusions of grandeur."[4] Thompson was right to connect Manning's personal struggles with her political struggles (as I discuss in chapter 3, Manning herself frames these struggles as connected), but Thompson's narrative paints this connection as politically problematic, portraying Manning's "private" motives as undermining any concern with the public good and undercutting the possible political promise of her act. When Manning's allies, such as Daniel Ellsberg, Glenn Greenwald, and Chase Madar, attempted to defend her, they did so by claiming that she was *not* motivated by private interest but instead by an interest in serving the public good.[5] Greenwald and Madar claimed she was following in the footsteps of Ellsberg, the famous Pentagon Papers whistleblower. These defenses were certainly politically important and valuable but they also assumed (like Thompson) that Manning's interest in drawing connections between public and private wrongs would be politically dangerous.

Manning's defenders and her many critics were, perhaps without realizing it, judging her actions in terms of a particular, historically situated, and politically produced conception of what a truth-teller looks like: someone who (like Socrates or Ellsberg) sets aside his private interest, publicly identifies himself as acting on behalf of the public good, and takes the consequences of telling an unpopular truth. While appealing to this heroic Socratic imaginary enables important defenses of truth-tellers, might it also narrow the kind of defenses of truth-telling we are able to make? If those who see something promising in Chelsea Manning's truth-telling stopped trying to make her into Daniel Ellsberg, how would she appear? What kind of example would she offer?

This book explores this question by positioning Manning's act differently, as following not in the footsteps of Socrates or Ellsberg but in the footsteps of Cassandra and her outsider collective. Like Cassandra, Manning's refusal to capitulate to the separation of public and private that her society sees as necessary to truthfulness is itself part of her truth-telling, even as it renders her untrustworthy in the eyes of her listeners. If Cassandra connected the violence of men over women to the violence of war and claimed that both would lead to Troy's ruin, I will suggest in chapter 3 that Manning connected the secrecy demanded by Don't Ask Don't Tell to the military secrecy of information about war.

As the book unfolds, I will put Manning into conversation not only with Cassandra, but also with Virginia Woolf, Audre Lorde, Bayard Rustin, and others. I will argue (especially in chapter 3) for reading her as an outsider truth-teller whose refusal to comply with norms of publicity and privacy render her illegible to her society as a truth-teller, while also putting her in a position to tell us important and unsettling truths about the public and private realms. While we tend to look to truth and truth-tellers to *re-stabilize* our political world and its public/private distinctions—by checking governmental corruption, or revealing the need for accountability—I will argue (especially in chapter 2) that outsider truth-tellers offer an important, *insurgent truth* to their societies. In contrast to the objective facts or moral absolutes that we tend to associate with truth-telling in politics, outsider truth-tellers suggest that our dominant understanding of "truth" as singular and absolute is itself complicit in oppression, and they offer a messier and more complex picture of what the world is like. Outsider truth-tellers do not seek to re-stabilize the world as it is, but instead to change it by creating spaces and connections where marginalized individuals can say what the world is like for them and begin to imagine how to make it otherwise.

In the remainder of this chapter, however, I aim to show why reading Manning as an outsider truth-teller, and developing a defense of outsider truth-telling, is important to our understanding of the relationship between democracy and truth more generally. I will suggest that outsider truth-telling reveals problems with, and offers an important alternative to, the dominant understanding of truth and democracy in political theory and public life, namely, the view that democracy is dependent on truth because it offers a prepolitical stability for a society of diverse viewpoints. While this understanding of truth seems so commonsensical as to be banal, I argue, through recourse to scholarship in the history of science, that it actually grew out of particular historical circumstances and is tied to a raced, classed, and gendered conception of what a truth-teller looks like. In this context, I will suggest that outsider truth-tellers should be understood as performing a distinct, important role for democracy: telling their fellow citizens that their sense of reality, and their sense of which problems call for political redress, is actually partial, overly simplified, and often reinforcing oppression. Revealing reality that their societies need to see from a position of social illegibility, outsider truth-tellers are crucial yet vulnerable figures for democracy who are often (as Chelsea Manning was and is) violently disciplined, punished, and ostracized rather than acknowledged and considered worthy of response. This chapter makes an argument for the importance of their role and suggests that the predicaments and problems surrounding outsider truth-telling are crucial ones for democratic theory to raise, thematize, and address.

TRUTH AND DEMOCRACY

In modern and contemporary political theory, theorists tend to portray truth as important to politics because it offers stability and a common ground for diverse opinions. For example, in her germinal essay, "Truth and Politics," Hannah Arendt argues that *factual* (as distinct from philosophical or religious) truth is an important source of stability for a diverse, free, contingent democratic politics.[6] Whereas religious and philosophical truths presume to reveal an essential human trait that ties us together—and hence may license the exercise of violence on those who do not appear to have that essential trait, or who believe in different truths—factual truth appears to have a validity distinct from how facts might be used or seen within broader theories or ideologies. As Arendt puts it, "Conceptually, we may call [factual] truth what we cannot change; metaphorically, it is the ground on which we stand and the sky that stretches above us."[7] Similarly, in *Truth and Truthfulness*, Bernard Williams argues that "everyday truths" and norms of truthfulness serve the important social function of stability.[8] Factual truth appears to offer a pre-political common ground upon which people of diverse views can stand and have a reasonable debate.

This intuitive connection between stable factual truths and democratic freedom is also evident in contemporary worries about our supposed descent into a "post-truth" age. Now almost two years (at the time of this writing) into the presidency of Donald Trump, whose administration has been marked by ongoing and brazen lying, popular political culture is filled with books and articles worrying about whether a loss of truthfulness in politics may herald an anti-democratic politics or even incipient authoritarianism or fascism. In the *Death of Truth: Notes on Falsehood in the Age of Trump*, Michiko Kakutani writes, for example, that "[t]ruth is a cornerstone of our democracy" and "[t]he assault on truth and reason" has "reached fever pitch in America during the first year of the Trump presidency."[9] Writing in the *New York Times* a few days before the election, Jason Stanley noted that "Trump . . . is an authoritarian using his speech to *define* a simple reality that legitimates his value system, leading voters to adopt it."[10] In a similar vein, the *Economist* writes that Trump's post-truth politics—which casts truth as of "secondary importance"—undermines the stability and commonality provided by factual truth: they "reinforce prejudices" and the disbelief of Trump's opponents "validates the us-versus-them mindset that outsider candidates thrive on."[11] Indeed, George Orwell's *1984*, which portrays factual truth as crucial to freedom, jumped onto the bestseller list after Trump's election. Orwell's depiction of a dystopian authoritarianism that defines its own "truth" suggests that without an available independent reality, about which citizens might form judgments and opinions, citizens' thoughts—like their bodies—are rendered deferent to their authoritarian rulers. They lose the capacity to critically depict a reality independent of what their rulers say it is.

These recent popular analyses of the threat lying poses to democracy are seductive because they imply that truth,

if properly respected, confers commonality without political work: that if we could only rid politics of liars, we
would restore the common ground (truth) that assures unity
amongst people of diverse viewpoints and, hence, democratic flourishing. Yet truth only appears in society and politics by virtue of a system of representation; and modern
systems of representing truth have been deeply hierarchical,
engendering an apparent commonality and unity for some,
and oppression and division for others.

As Mary Poovey, Steven Shapin, and other historians of
science show, the idea of "facts" as self-evident and transparent
itself arose in modernity out of hierarchy: through systems
of representation that excluded certain kinds of experience,
testimony, and speakers. For example, as Shapin argues in
A Social History of Truth, while the early moderns claimed
that "[t]he legitimate springs of empirical knowledge were
located in the individual's sensory confrontation with the
world,"[12] they also saw certain representations of credibility
as more convincing than others. In particular, Shapin argues
that the question of *which* representations of facts were credible was answered by the early moderns through reference to
the existing status of "gentlemen": "[p]articipants 'just knew'
who a credible person was. They belonged to a culture that
pointed to gentlemen as among their society's most reliable
truth-tellers, a culture that associated gentility, integrity, and
credibility."[13] As Shapin puts it, "[i]n certain sorts of people
credibility was *embodied*."[14]

If Shapin argues that early modern scientists encoded
credibility as a set of gentlemanly virtues, Poovey suggests
that the idea of a nugget of experience *as* credible (as a "fact")
was first produced through a particular form of early modern
merchants' writing practices: double-entry bookkeeping.[15]

While this "formal system of writing numbers" transformed risky transactions "into usable facts"[16] by recording them in a rule-bound way (mathematically) that *appears* to "guarantee accuracy,"[17] this "formal precision" took the place of, and literally rewrote, the initial recordings of transactions that were often by a "woman or a young person." These individuals' representations of the transactions were not credible because they wrote, in the words of a manual on double-entry book-keeping, "after the capacities of their minds."[18] Hiding and transcribing this first recording, the conventions of double-entry bookkeeping not only obscured conditions of risk in business but also produced particular ways of thinking *as* risky and not credible: women and young people were portrayed as incapable of the rule-governed writing necessary to generate the self-evident particular.[19]

The "fact" is not, then, the nugget of raw experience we often take it to be, but a form of representing reality governed by strict rules (of writing) that produce its supposed self-evidence. And this form of representing reality is itself premised on a hierarchy of credibility: the formal precision of male merchants is privileged over the direct experience of women and young people.[20]

Poovey and Shapin's work thus suggests that modern conceptions of credibility depend on a system of representation that casts certain "nuggets of individual experience" (precise, ordered, stripped of "excess") as hearable as facts, and certain kinds of speakers (male merchants and gentlemen) and speech (civil, decorous) as offering hearable testimony about those facts. Further, Poovey emphasizes that this account of truth filled a social and political need for stability and objectivity, in the new context of reason-of-state theories, which portrayed society as composed of warring interests.[21] Yet Poovey's and Shapin's accounts also reveal that these early modern practices of truth generate a particular idea of what stability and objectivity *are*, and how they are represented: for example, objectivity becomes identifiable through rule-governed practices of representing reality, and stability appears as a situation of acquiescence to gendered, raced, and economic hierarchy. Here, as Leigh Gilmore writes in a different context, we see "objectivity's alignment against the dispossessed."[22]

Contemporary critics of a "post-truth era" appear to be operating from within the parameters of this early modern model: where truth-telling is supposed to create unity by serving as a site of rule-governed objectivity and disinterestedness, produced by expertly curated information deemed publicly significant by elites. In this model, the person who can speak this truth and offer it to society must himself appear capable of objectivity, disinterestedness, and maintaining distance from the private sphere (all features that align with gendered, raced, and elite traits).

While this early modern model of the relationship between truth and politics might appear to offer stability (an appearance I will later put into question), I am suggesting that it may also be anti-democratic: rendering marginalized speakers *and* unsettling truths about oppression and inequality always already insignificant to the public realm. This anti-democratic character persists. We can see it, for example, in the divergent public, journalistic, and legislative responses to Chelsea Manning's and Edward Snowden's leaking of documents. Both Manning and Snowden leaked what we would call evidence or "facts," consisting in official governmental records that include documents and video. No one has disputed the authenticity or veracity of what either

Manning or Snowden released to the public. Yet the information leaked by Manning and Snowden has been taken up in very different ways. While the information leaked by Manning was picked up by journalists, who used it to give the public a broader picture of US war-making and diplomacy,[23] the public and legislators were muted and mostly negative in their initial response to Manning's actions. In contrast, the information leaked by Snowden was seen as politically significant by both citizens and legislators. Snowden's actions sparked bipartisan legislative attempts to curb the National Security Agency's powers and authority, as well as citizen outrage over their breached privacy.[24] In addition, Snowden himself has become something of a hero in leftist circles and a *cause célèbre*. The American Civil Liberties Union (ACLU), for instance, mounted a massive "Pardon Snowden" campaign at the end of President Obama's term, which was supported by public intellectuals and law professors, as well as by celebrities like Mark Ruffalo and Maggie Gyllenhal. In addition to participating in a documentary by Laura Poitras while he leaked the documents, Snowden was also the subject of an Oliver Stone biopic. While Manning certainly has a fervent base of supporters, which increased in number during her time in prison, she has never sparked the large-scale public fervor and admiration that has followed Snowden; and the admiration Manning *has* attracted has largely focused on her as a person (and as a trans* person who has fought for adequate treatment in prison), rather than on the information she leaked.[25]

Certainly, these divergent responses to Snowden and Manning can in part be accounted for by reference to perceptions of Manning as a less credible speaker. Whereas Manning is sexually and gender non-conforming, and portrayed herself as spurred to act by both public and private motives, Snowden portrayed himself in the Poitras documentary as typically masculine, heterosexual, and motivated purely by a concern with a narrow public good: privacy. While we learned a great deal about Manning's private life when she was discovered as the leaker, virtually nothing about Snowden's private life appeared in the mainstream press,[26] and it was not the central part of the public narrative about him. Thus, it was easy for him to portray himself as telling the truth purely on behalf of the public good. Without a doubt, the different (liberal/Left) public response to the two leakers—turning Snowden into a hero and relegating Manning to the background—was rooted in part in perception of Snowden as a more credible public speaker and actor than Manning.

Yet the facts that Snowden revealed were also more easily spoken and heard *as* truth than the facts revealed by Manning. The truth Snowden told—that privacy must be respected and kept separate from public and political ends—harmonized with the role he had to occupy in order to be seen as a truth-teller: someone who is able to distance himself from and sacrifice private interests and feelings (not telling his girlfriend he plans to leak information and leave the country and preparing to sacrifice his relationship) on behalf of the public good of *keeping the private, private.* Put differently, the facts that Snowden revealed appeared to show a way in which the government had wrongly destabilized the private realm and, by revealing them, Snowden sought to re-stabilize public *and* private life, to restore the proper boundary between them—just as he also did in his very performance of truth-telling. In contrast, Manning's leaks suggest that abuses in US diplomacy and war are not exceptions that need to be remedied so that government can be restored to its proper public function; rather, they suggest that these abuses pervade the US government and raise the question of whether supposedly legitimate and just norms of governance are actually corrupt and require more radical transformation. Rather than restoring stability and the proper line between public and private, Manning's truths question and unsettle the proper line between public and private.

I am suggesting here that Manning's example, read in conjunction with Snowden's, reveals in part a problem of social and political illegibility, that people who are telling the truths society most needs to hear are those that appear in-credible to that society. Yet Manning's example also reflects the problem I drew out in my discussion of Shapin and Poovey's work: that dominant public models of truth and credibility render certain speakers and certain kinds of truth always already insignificant. In other words, the problem revealed in the divergent public responses to Manning and Snowden may be not *only* that a particular model of credibility keeps us from hearing speakers who tell us things we need to hear, but also that a certain notion of truth is linked to that sense of credibility, and helps keep it in place. In particular, when we think of truth as something that offers prepolitical stability, we may tend to see speakers whose truths appear to unsettle that stability as less credible, and vice versa. Thus, to render Manning's truths hearable as politically significant, we may not only need to develop a more sensitive receptivity to marginalized speakers—as thinkers like Iris Marion Young and Miranda Frick have rightly argued[27]. Rather, we may also need to put dominant models of the relation between truth and democracy into question, and examine how those models help to sustain certain forms of hierarchy and exclusivity.

Yet my aim is not to suggest that the modern factual truth-teller—or the facts he or she tells—should be discarded. Rather, my argument is that the question of how societies create and understand the socio-political role of truth-teller should be a critical project of social and political theory. In this claim, I build on Michel Foucault's work in his late lectures on *parrhesia*, where he suggests that giving attention to the socially and politically constituted *role* of the truth-teller reveals an alternative approach to the problem of truth. In lectures at the College de France and in his series of lectures at University of California Berkeley published as *Fearless Speech*, Foucault argues for a turn away from "the problem of truth" and toward the "problem of the truth-teller, or of truth-telling as an activity"[28]—that is, as he puts it in *The Courage of Truth*, toward the project of "analyz[ing] the conditions and forms of the type of act by which the subject *manifests* himself when speaking the truth, by which I mean, thinks of himself and is recognized by others as speaking the truth."[29] In contrast to philosophers focused on what Foucault calls "the analytics of truth"[30] who attempt to articulate "the criteria for true statements and sound reasoning," writers (like Foucault) interested in the "question of truth from the point of view of truth-telling as an activity" ask questions like: "Who is able to tell the truth? What are the moral, the ethical, and the spiritual conditions which entitle someone to present himself as, and to be considered as, a truth-teller?"[31] This "critical" approach to truth-telling[32] reveals that no form of veridiction is absolute and that forms of truth-telling—as Poovey and Shapin show in terms of modern forms of credibility—are historically and politically conditioned in different ways in different times and places. From this perspective, the analytics of truth, which presents itself as objectively identifying criteria for assessing or speaking truth, appears as itself always partial, since it operates within a historically and politically constituted understanding of the nature of truth and truth-telling.

Insofar as I am interested in "truth-telling as an activity" and the social and political conditions that enable someone to count as a truth-teller, I follow Foucault's "critical" approach to truth-telling. Yet I also depart from Foucault in two primary ways. Where Foucault's examination of *parrhesia* in Greco-Roman culture tends to focus on dominant or already legible forms of truth-telling, I am more interested in alternative or marginalized forms of truth-telling—forms that Foucault tends to overlook in the texts he interprets in the lectures.[33] Second, Foucault's greatest interest in his lectures is in a dyadic or individual form of *parrhesia* that consists in an ethical art of the self. He calls this form of *parrhesia* philosophical *parrhesia* and associates it with Socrates, the Stoics, and the Cynics. While Foucault's contemporary interpreters look to his account of philosophical *parrhesia* as offering a practice able to release the individual from the subjection characteristic of disciplinary and bio-power,[34] their focus on individual or dyadic ethical practices of undoing and remaking the self also blind us to their enmeshment in social and political hierarchies of truth, where some people are seen as able to engage in ethical practices of truth-telling and others not. To look to ethical practices of truth-telling as a route to political emancipation offers, as Ella Myers argues,[35] individual solace in situations of political disempowerment but fails to address the political context that creates disempowerment for some groups more than others.

This book thus calls us to critically examine how we understand what truth-telling could or should offer to politics.

Yet the book also aims in particular to draw attention to the democratic significance of outsider truth-telling, and to suggest that certain forms of political contest over truth may be productive and not just damaging for democratic politics. Truth-telling *may* offer important facts to politics that generate stability, but truth-tellers may also perform a crucial function by unsettling the supposed common ground, and revealing it to be partial and oppressive. If the problem of the dominant form of truth-telling is that the passions of the demos (perhaps as the result of the efforts of other elites to "spin" perception through propaganda or sophistry) may blind it to the self-evident truth being told, then the problem of outsider truth-telling is that dominant social codes portray outsiders and their truths as always already in-credible. The difference here is between seeing the problem in terms of *democratic incompetence*—the susceptibility of the masses to lies—and seeing the problem in a broader set of factors (e.g., capitalism, technology, patriarchy, heteronormativity, white supremacy, and what Saidiya Hartmann has called the "afterlife of slavery"[36]) that enable certain political scenes, truths, and individuals to be staged as credible, and others as in-credible.

TRUTH AND SECURITY

The outsider truth-tellers I examine in this book diagnose, reveal, and sometimes unsettle a dominant system of representing truth. I will suggest in the chapters that follow that this dominant system, which overlaps with but is not wholly coincident with, the regime of the modern fact, is constituted by three primary characteristics. While these

characteristics will unfold in greater depth as the book pro-
ceeds, I outline them here in schematic fashion and then
outline the practice and world that outsider truth-telling
counterposes to them.

First, outsider truth-tellers suggest that our dominant
system of representing truth is shaped by a broader security
regime (e.g., modern capitalism and militarism, violence in
the name of "security," digital technology, patriarchy). This
truth-security regime demands, and renders hearable and
significant, truths and truth-tellers that *appear* to offer stability and security, namely, speakers whose truth-telling *limits
risk, sustains the status quo, contains "threats,"* and *enables
strategic prediction.* Truth-security regimes are not devoid of
crisis and often use crises to bolster and sustain the felt need
for security.[37] The power of such regimes is the image of security they proffer, an image that links security with a particular style of credibility (masculine, rule-governed, precise).
Of course, for many people who appear in-credible within
such regimes, this image of security actually creates great
*in*security, in the form of oppression and privation. While
the image of the contemporary truth-security regime that
emerges in this book certainly appears as a version of neoliberalism or what Gilles Deleuze calls the "control society,"
the distinctive contribution outsider truth-tellers make is
to show that an exclusive *system of credibility* (some parts
of which may also be useful and productive) underlies and
sustains the contemporary control society.

Second, while many political theorists have responded
to the privatization indicative of neoliberalism by inci-
sively urging us to rejuvenate a democratic concern with the
public good, or with "public things,"[38] outsider truth-tellers
portray the private *and* public realms, and especially the

claim of a separation between them, as linked sites of domination. Categorizing some people as fit to appear in public and others as suited to the private sphere; portraying some interests as properly public and others as private; these are all means by which hierarchy (as many feminist and queer thinkers have long suggested) is sustained. Outsider truthtellers also indict the public realm as indelibly connected to violence: the physical violence of the police, military, and fathers and husbands, as well as the psychological and interpersonal violence of silencing, diminishing, and marginalizing individuals in everyday life. As crucial institutions in a regime of hierarchical legibility, violence, and dominance, outsider truth-tellers indict both the public and private realms as fundamentally oppressive.

Finally, I see outsider truth-telling as confronting what I call a *hermeneutic circle of credibility* in our modern truthsecurity regime: speakers are considered credible when they are able to tell a particular kind of truth (narrow, precise, abstract, "self-evident"), but statements are considered true only when they are told by particular kinds of speakers (masculine, materially comfortable, sexually and gender conforming, white). This hermeneutic circle works to make the circle of credibility *appear* to be expandable (if you can tell us "facts," if you obtain video footage of a police shooting, if you have witnesses to a rape, etc., you will be believed and your reality taken seriously), while at the same time sealing it closed in practice since facts can, within this circle, only appear if they sustain existing hierarchies, and be spoken by already credible individuals. This hermeneutic circle also demands that marginalized individuals become, or aspire to become, different kinds of people, if they are to be received as credible; yet in practice, this assimilation to dominant norms will always be imperfect. They will try to change who they are but will never be taken as fully trustworthy.

Opposed to this security-truth regime, outsider truth-tellers counterpose their own practices and the outsider world they are at work in creating: a world that attempts to create stability and security not through depending on the violent protection of the state but through creating connections and alternative forms of legibility with other outsiders. I identify three primary features of this alternative form of truth-telling, which I describe as generating *insurgent truth*: truth that does not order society from a position of transcendence but instead is part of a creative attempt to reveal—and change—the messy, complex, complicated truth of a patriarchal, hierarchical, militaristic world.

First, rather than seeking to reclaim or rework publicity—as in Michael Warner's "counterpublics"—these outsider truth-tellers mostly seek to create new kinds of spaces and languages that refuse the terms of *both* public and private spheres, *even if or when* they speak to those realms. Put differently, they respond to the hermeneutic circle of credibility not by trying to break or transform it, but instead, and as I discuss in more detail in chapter 2, by transforming and creating spaces where it does not apply: spaces where outsiders might work at constructing a new world in which they and their truths will appear significant. While I examine the tensions and limits of this kind of practice throughout the book, their rejection and questioning of this core precept of modern (and postmodern) political theory offers an example of how *refusing publicity* can be a meaningful, world-building practice.

Second, in contrast to democratic theorists' focus on *political subjectivity*—the claiming or creation of a new subjectivity or identity through political action (Jacques Ranciere, Arendt)—as an (ambivalent) site of emancipation, outsider truth-tellers are instead preoccupied with *anonymity* as a social and political form that unsettles and calls into question all forms of identity. In chapter 4, I read outsider anonymity as a practice that does not reflect a desire to escape notice but rather is a positive expression of the limits of public and private norms of recognition. Refusing to be recognized in the terms of publicity, anonymity—as either a *signature* that generates an alternative archive or a *routine* that generates an outsider repertoire (Diana Taylor)—creates a material and imagined space distinct from public and private where outsider truth-telling can be performed and gain significance.

Finally, outsider truth-tellers refuse to narrate the truths they tell, that is, to put those truths into a broader narrative that makes sense of them for their audience and issues a clear call to action. Instead, they tend to *leak* truth, to disseminate truth without trying to control where it ends up, in hopes that they might create new connections with other outsiders and—perhaps—generate hitherto unknown associations and worlds. As I discuss in chapter 5, the practice of leaking reveals that the system *can* leak, that there are already cracks and spaces within the public and private realms that are not controlled or determined by their norms and thus are available for outsider transformation and creativity.

Through these practices, outsider truth-tellers do not abandon but rather create a different kind of security: not the fantasy of a prepolitical common ground but instead a creative form of solidarity that seeks to achieve rather than presume a difficult commonality.

COUNTER-ARCHIVE
AND REPERTOIRE

The group of outsider truth-tellers I examine in this book is a constructed group, to which I turn for two primary reasons. First, I will suggest in the chapters that follow that this assemblage of thinkers and actors generates productive insights and re-orientations about truth and politics for contemporary theorists and political actors. Rather than accepting the premise that (credible) truth offers security *qua* certainty or a prepolitical "common ground" to politics, these thinkers and actors reveal this premise as complicit in the oppressions of a war society and offer an alternative conception of how outsider truth-telling might productively aid democratic politics: by articulating insurgent truths, spaces, and connections that make a more equitable, freer world possible.

Second, I turn to these figures because the alternative model of truth-telling I develop out of their writings and actions is a model, I argue, that we need in our contemporary moment. Chelsea Manning is at the center of this story not because she is a *better* truth-teller than Cassandra or Bayard Rustin or Virginia Woolf, but because the way in which we see her example matters a great deal for contemporary politics. If we see her as the mainstream press suggests that we see her—as a failed whistleblower who has become a compelling spokesperson for trans* justice issues—we assume that truth-telling is only significant and meaningful when truth-tellers conform to dominant models of credibility (which many of us may never be able to inhabit successfully in any case). However, if we see her as I argue we should—as an outsider who tells an *insurgent truth* that we need to hear, even if it unsettles our way of living—then the possibility of resisting dominant, marginalizing truth regimes becomes more of a live possibility, one that we might emulate, politically respond to, or take up creatively in other ways.

To describe the kind of grouping of thinkers and writers I am pursuing, I borrow Kathi Weeks's description of a "counter-archive."[39] Whereas a tradition is something we inherit and which stands as a legitimating basis for our forms of thought, speech, and actions, Weeks argues that to "gather together" materials to create an archive is "itself something of an act, a provocation, an argument, or at least the staging of an event that might inspire these things."[40] The point of an archive, in other words, is not to stand as a firm "foundation" on which new knowledge may be based, but rather to create new temporalities, sets of resonances, and sites of meaning. As Weeks says, "[t]he specific generativity of an archive comes from the resonances of its parts. Its force depends on what each text amplifies in the others, how reading them in proximity to one another produces new insights as they build on and reformulate shared themes and commitments or when their occasional differences are magnified such that the disruption they instigate assumes new meaning."[41] In putting Cassandra, Woolf, Lorde, Rustin, and Manning in conversation with each other, I thus aim not to create a "tradition" of outsider truth-telling which will legitimate future outsider truth-tellers. Rather, I aim to reveal new meanings and resonances in all of these figures, and create a network of meaning in which other acts of outsider truth-telling appear significant.

I also do not call outsider truth-telling a "tradition" because I want to emphasize the important differences among the figures I examine. For example, Woolf, Rustin, Lorde, and Manning all practice outsider truth-telling in different historical moments, via distinct media, and from different subject positions: as a non-sexually conforming white woman, a black gay Quaker man, a lesbian Black woman, and a trans* white woman. Their distinct predicaments shape the character of their outsider truth-telling: in terms, for example, of the degree and manner in which they refuse publicity, in the kind of outsider spaces and practices they imagine and enact, and in the kind of truth they seek to tell. Thus, in seeking to illustrate *resonances* in a counter-archive rather than arguing for the *continuity* of a tradition, I aim to emphasize how the different practices of truth-telling I examine here may—without erasing the differences among these truth-tellers and the truths they tell—create a synergistic world where other outsider practices of truth-telling gain significance and appear more possible and meaningful.

Creating a counter-archive of outsider truth-telling also generates what Brittney Cooper calls an "intellectual geography." In her important book, *Beyond Respectability*, Cooper argues that taking "Black women seriously as thinkers and knowledge producers" means that "we must begin to look for their thinking in unexpected places": "in genres like autobiography, novels, news stories, medical records, organizational histories, public speeches and diary entries."[42] Those who are not groomed and enshrined in conventional locations of academic writing and knowledge production will inevitably do their thinking elsewhere and, often, otherwise. Drawing on "an unexpected" and "eclectic archive,"[43] Cooper highlights how the thinking of race women from the 1890s to the 1970s depends on the creation of spaces—for example, the creation of the National Colored Women's Association—that stand outside of or in tension with dominant public spaces.

In this book, the counter-archive I generate reveals an "intellectual geography" of outsider truth-telling that includes creative practices and solidarities within pacifist organizations, online chats, prisons, poetry, ordinary domestic spaces, and bridges and corners (among others). The outsider spaces that appear in this geography produce material that we can find in the archive, but they were also produced by what Diana Taylor calls the "repertoire." If the archive contains "documents, maps, literary texts, letters, archaeological remains, bones, videos, films, CDs, all those items supposedly resistant to change," the repertoire "enacts embodied memory: performances, gestures, orality, movement, dance, singing—in short, all those acts usually thought of as ephemeral, nonreproducible knowledge."[44] Emphasizing that the repertoire is more stable than we tend to think and the archive more changeable,[45] Taylor suggests that archive and repertoire are not opposites, but rather "systems of transmission" and "important sources of information, both exceeding the limitation of the other, in literate and semi-literate societies."[46]

I take outsider repertoire, and not just outsider texts that we find in the archive, seriously as a site of meaning, world-building, and truth-telling because it reminds us of the mutual dependence of material traces of outsider life and the maintenance of a live repertoire of outsider truth-telling. We only have a counter-archive of outsider truth-telling because outsiders continue to rehearse, perform, change, and re-perform/rehearse ways of telling the truth and creating spaces where that truth can be heard and lent significance, and vice versa.

Generating and drawing together a counter-archive and repertoire of outsider truth-telling is a practice that has a politics. Through connecting thinkers, writers, and actors across time, and drawing out resonances between them as outsider truth-tellers, this book calls us to see all of them through the lens of each other's thinking and examples— that is, to see them anew. If I find in outsider truth-telling an important practice of unsettling an exclusive imaginary of truth and truth-telling, my construction of the particular counter-archive and repertoire that will unfold in this book is aimed at encouraging us, as I discuss in more detail in the concluding chapter, to consider contemporary dilemmas of truth and democracy differently.

In what follows, I first (in chapter 2) make an argument for the importance of outsider truth-telling as offering a distinctive conception of truth-telling: the practice of *refusing* the public/private divide that structures norms of proper speech and comportment. As I have been suggesting in this chapter, outsider truth-telling reveals a reality of oppression and domination that productively unsettles society, but I will suggest in chapter 2 that it also enables, and is perhaps necessary to, outsider survival and flourishing. Yet this outsider practice of truth-telling is also inhabited by a dilemma: how to maintain a capacity to speak truth *to* the public and private realms (and be heard by them) that depends at the same time on remaining outside of those realms in some sense. I argue that the creation and imagination of tenuous outsider spaces (I focus in particular on Virginia Woolf's "bridge" and Anna Julia Cooper's "corner") offer a promising way to negotiate this dilemma and create a political imaginary in which one need not be *absorbed* by public and private realms in order to speak to them.

In chapter 3, I build on this conception of outsider truth-telling to examine Chelsea Manning's leaking of documents.

The chapter argues for reading Manning in terms of a new category: what I call a "transformative truth-teller." Through close examination of the chat logs between Manning and Adrian Lamo—chat logs which Lamo turned over to the Federal Bureau of Investigation (FBI)—I argue that we should value rather than dismiss the connections Manning makes between, on the one hand, her "private" struggles with Don't Ask Don't Tell (the US Army policy that mandated the secrecy of her gender and sexuality) and, on the other hand, her struggles with mandated secrecy of information about government abuses of power in the Iraq and Afghanistan wars. I read Manning's truth-telling, and her connection between public and private, as not simply an attempt to state or reveal facts but also as an enactment of herself, as a non-gender-conforming person, resistant to the US Army's articulation of the national interest, as a proper speaker and defender of that public good. Yet her leaking, I argue, aims not to *restore* institutions to normal functioning, but rather to *transform* those institutions and the world so that she and her truths can be heard and seen as significant.

In chapter 4, I take Manning's attempt to leak these documents *anonymously* as a springboard to examine the promise of anonymity as an outsider practice. Anonymous leaking is typically depicted as a problem for democracy because its breach of governmental security protocols requires a justification that cannot be provided because of the leaker's anonymity, which also hinders the demos from judging an individual's motives and truthfulness. However, I argue, through discussion of Wendy Hui Kyong Chun's work, as well as discussion of Woolf and Rustin, that outsiders' refusals to identify themselves in public or private terms can also signal the failure of those terms to capture them and the significance of their speech. Anonymity on my reading can thus be a positive *marker* of an experience that exceeds public and private norms of recognition. I suggest that either through using a signature, such as Anon., or engaging in practices of what I call, using the work of Kevin Quashie, "quiet persistence" (Rustin), outsiders can create counterarchives and repertoires in the context of which other outsiders may find their own significance better illuminated. Read in this way, Manning's anonymity—which she explains as necessary so that her picture will not be plastered everywhere "as a boy"—should be read not as an attempt to avoid public justification or punishment but instead as a marker of the insufficiency of public categories to capture her experience, identity, and act.

Chapter 5 explores concretely how Manning's leaking of what came to be known as the *Collateral Murder* video may have changed, or may be at work in changing, the world. I explore this question by framing the video's import in terms of Virginia Woolf's discussion of war photographs in *Three Guineas*. My contention is that the revealing or display of photographs, as well as moving images, can transform various functional sites (offices, sitting rooms, work computers) into sites of truth-telling and, in turn, into sites for challenges to hierarchy, by empowering, enabling, or even demanding the speech and truths of new speakers. As an example of this, I focus in particular on the story of Ethan McCord, a US Army infantryman who appears in the *Collateral Murder* video rushing to pick up the children injured by the shooting from the Army helicopter. Prompted by the release of *Collateral Murder*, McCord began giving interviews (and appearing in a documentary) about that incident—which haunts him—and about his broader view of the damage the US Army's presence is doing both to Iraqis and to Americans (and, in particular, to himself). McCord's voice solicited other voices of US soldiers opposed to war. Manning's leaking of this video footage should thus be read as world-changing insofar as it created spaces where the speech of soldiers like McCord, critical of war, was enabled and demanded.

In the last chapter, I ask what the counter-archive and repertoire I draw out might have to teach us about our contemporary political moment. Specifically, I ask: if the self-evidence of facts is actually produced by a dominant *system of representing truth*, is it more politically productive to see ourselves as entering a "post-truth era," or to instead see ourselves as living in a moment when a modern ideal of dispassionate speakers of rational truth is in crisis and when this ideal and the system of representation it underwrites no longer seem to be working or offering stability to the political realm? Described as the latter, we might be able to see Trump's version of dismissing facts as one nodal point in a broader crisis of representation, which may contain sites of political danger *and* political promise. If our system of representing truth is in crisis, perhaps rather than throwing up our hands and saying we are in a "post-truth" age, we would do better to examine what precedents and examples of other, possibly more democratic or emancipatory, models of truth-telling might already be at work around us on which we might draw to rethink what truth-telling does, and might do, for politics. I thematize one such model that I find in Manning's prison writings: even in the most disciplinary situations, outsider connections may be at work in creating new scenes of reality into which we might enter and pleasurably re-orient ourselves to and create spaces through which we might better address the violences and oppressions of our world.

PUBLIC,

PRIVATE, INSURGENT

What Is Outsider Truth-Telling?

IF MUCH OF THE GOAL of modern and contemporary political theory has been to properly adjudicate the line between private and public, outsiders experience this line as
part of a political system that subjugates them. Appearing
as improper figures in both public and private, outsiders see
these realms as linked sites of militarism, patriarchy, racism,
heteronormativity, and capitalism. The damage exerted on
all of us by this division, which outsiders experience most
keenly and with the most devastating cost, is that we become
fractured political subjects, constantly working to be appropriate figures in both public and private realms, for the sake
of (among other things) economic security, love, and political respect, while also experiencing recognition (for good
and ill) in public and private as oppressive and hierarchical.

Outsiders enact themselves as "outside" systems of oppression in which they also reside by identifying public and
private as dual sites of oppression, and they sound notes of
caution (and opposition) to attempts of the marginalized to

be assimilated into those realms. In Audre Lorde's terms, outsiders see that the "master's tools" will never free the oppressed from the "master's house," but will instead bind marginalized peoples more firmly to systems of oppression.

While outsider thinking and politics have much to offer to a broad variety of political and theoretical concerns, I am particularly interested in this chapter in identifying the role of truth-telling in outsider practice and politics. Through drawing on thinkers and writers like Lorde, Virginia Woolf, Anna Julia Cooper, and Adrienne Rich, I will suggest that outsider truth-telling works as a practice of *identifying* the oppressive, linked character of both public and private realms and in turn identifying oneself as in some sense an outsider *to* those realms. Outsiders refuse the terms of both public and private precisely through telling the truth about them. This refusal bears similarities to the refusal of the prophet who, as George Shulman has argued, indicts the corruption of their society on behalf of redemption, either through rebirth, returning to first principles of equality, freedom, or justice, or accepting our implication in oppression.[1] Yet while some outsider truth-telling may solicit or call for redemption, I focus here on how outsider truth-telling has value as a practice of generating *new* forms of truthfulness and collectivity. Indeed, the enactment of outsider truth-telling is itself the revelation of a real, live possibility of another way of living, where truth and art, rather than war and oppression, are primary values. Outsider truth-telling here becomes a practice of *sur*-vival (survival as flourishing, excess life), where telling the truth is a way to make connections with other outsiders and maintain a sense of outsider significance in a world that tells them that they do not understand their own reality.

The outsider commitment to truth-telling as a practice that reveals reality *and* forges connection, that enables outsider survival/flourishing *and* the survival of their society, generates a distinctive dilemma: how to be seen and heard by other outsiders and perhaps even a public audience while refusing public and private terms of visibility and audibility that distort the outsider's person and the truth they tell, and also threaten their survival. While there are many ways outsiders might negotiate this dilemma, I focus on the practice (that I find in Woolf, Cooper, and others) of imagining and creating outsider spaces, where outsiders can speak to and within a public realm without being absorbed by it. I focus in particular on Woolf's image of "the bridge" and Cooper's depiction of herself in the "corner" of the public realm. Through relating to the public and private realms from a space that cannot be fully captured by them, outsider truth-telling enacts, and leaves open the possibility of, *change*: political, personal, and everything in between.[2]

Before I turn to the dilemma of outsider truth-telling, however, I first develop a conception of outsider truth-telling as a practice of refusal, connection, and flourishing. I do so through staging a debate between Woolf's portrayal of outsider truth-telling as an individual capacity produced through gendered exclusion and Lorde's and other Black feminists' depictions of outsider truth-telling as a *non-sovereign* capacity that is nurtured through difficult conversations among outsiders. Woolf's concept of the outsider carves out an important critical space through which to reveal the imbrications between militarism, patriarchy, and capitalism. However, I argue that Lorde's concept of non-sovereign outsider truth-telling productively allows us to understand the importance of collective outsider engagement, talk, and action in enabling marginalized individuals to trust their own perceptions of reality in the context of multiple racialized and gendered forms of oppression.

OUTSIDER TRUTH-TELLING: REFUSAL, CONNECTION, FLOURISHING

In 1938, Virginia Woolf published *Three Guineas*, in which she argues that the seeds of fascism lie not in some foreign Italian or German essence but in patriarchal and militaristic ways of life that also pervade Britain and the rest of Europe. Highlighting the similarities between the fascist dictator, British professionals of all stripes, and the father in the domestic home, Woolf argues that the battle for freedom and equality lies not just in actual war with fascist leaders and nations (e.g., the Spanish Civil War) but also and perhaps more primarily in the fight against patriarchy, capitalism, and militarism at home. While Woolf appreciates the work of pacifist men on this score, she suggests that perhaps the most important form of resistance to patriarchal militarism is open only to women. This is because women's subordinate status in the private realm, and their exclusion from the professions and the military, gives them the capacity to be "Outsiders" to both public and private realms: to see and tell the truth about war, patriarchy, and fascism in ways that those invested in patriarchal militarism cannot.

For Woolf, women become outsiders when they come to consciousness about a capacity for truth-telling that they already have by virtue of their exclusion. Indeed, she re-stages women's exclusion as generative of greater objectivity than that possessed by professional men. For Woolf, *inclusion* within these realms obscures rather than illuminates reality. To become a successful professional, Woolf says, means that men literally "lose their senses" (*TG*, 72). To achieve money and status, "[y]ou will have to perform some duties that are very arduous, others that are very barbarous. You will have to wear certain uniforms and profess certain loyalties. If you succeed in those professions the words 'For God and the Empire' will very likely be written, like the address on a dog-collar, round your neck" (70).[3] Motivated by professional and material reward, even professional (supposed) truth-tellers – such as professors, journalists, and doctors – learn to see the complexity of human lives in terms of hierarchical categories that serve patriarchal, imperial/militaristic, and capitalist systems of domination. By portraying certain sets of individuals—women, non-Europeans, and (to a certain degree) the lower classes—as naturally unfit to enter the public realm of the professions and politics, expert truth-tellers ensure that the prerogatives of elite men stay intact. Producing categories and classifications, these experts create "facts" that elites can use to rule.[4]

In contrast to this professional, masculine inability to see reality, Woolf suggests (in part through her own example) that women's forced disinvestment in patriarchy, militarism, and capitalism gives them the capacity to see and speak the truth. For Woolf, however, exclusion does not generate the capacity for truth-telling because it settles women in a maternal role in the domestic realm that keeps them closer to reality than men (a position associated with standpoint theorists like Nancy Hartsock and Sara Ruddick[5]). Indeed, Woolf suggests—foreshadowing the work of queer theorists such as Michael Warner and Eve Sedgwick[6]—that the norms and mores of the private sphere are actually formed by the hierarchies of the public sphere. Woolf says: it is "[y]our world . . . , the world of professional life"—the world of "preaching, money-making, administering justice"—from which "the private house . . . has derived its creeds, its laws, its clothes and carpets, its beef and mutton" (*TG*, 23).[7] Depicting the private home as a scene of domination and violence, rather than a truthful reprieve from it, Woolf suggests that women's exclusion gives them the capacity for truth-telling because of the characterological *traits* the experience of exclusion cultivates in them. Indeed, Woolf urges outsiders to hold on to, nurture, and revalue characteristics that were initially the result of privation but may also contribute to outsider (and human) flourishing. For example, Woolf describes an enforced "mental chastity" (*TG*, 99)—the inability to sell one's brain for money—that can aid women in sustaining their outsider ability to see reality more clearly. A capacity (here, for writing and thinking) that is inoperative in patriarchy becomes repurposed for outsider flourishing.[8]

Despite her solicitation in *Three Guineas* of women as outsider truth-tellers, Woolf sees most women of her class ("daughters of educated men") as active participants in patriarchal militarism: for example, by supporting their brothers who fight in wars, working in hospitals during wars, or simply by affirming their role as domestic support for professional men. Yet she also finds, and brings to her readers' attention, multiple examples of women who refused to be complicit in their private or (non-)public roles: writers, doctors, mayoresses, scientists, women in sports. And in writing *Three Guineas*, Woolf herself enacts the practice of outsider truth-telling as a refusal of the norms of the public and private realms in which she is also enmeshed. In so doing, she reveals the possibility that those marginalized and oppressed by the war society *need not* consent to its narration of who they are and that they might, through telling the truth, restage their own value.

Later Black feminist accounts of outsider status similarly portray marginalization as offering a capacity for a clearer outsider vision, while also stressing that white women may be more invested in patriarchal militarism than Woolf sees or realizes. For example, in her account of Black feminist scholars as "outsiders within," Patricia Hill Collins says that "where traditional sociologists," including white women, "may see sociology as 'normal' and define their role as furthering knowledge about a normal world with taken-for-granted assumptions, outsiders within are liable to see anomalies." In particular, "Afro-American female scholars are repeatedly struck by their own invisibility, both as full human subjects included in sociological facts and observations, and as practitioners in the discipline itself."[9] Similarly, bell hooks argues "[i]t is essential for continued feminist struggle that black women recognize the special vantage point our marginality gives us and make use of their perspective to criticize the dominant racist, classist, sexist hegemony as well as to envision and create a counter-hegemony."[10] Where Woolf sees gendered exclusion as generating a capacity for truth-telling, hooks, Collins, and others draw attention to how white women may be invested in systems of patriarchy and militarism and learn to see reality through a lens of racial hierarchy that hides the reality of the oppression of black women, as well as the possibilities for human flourishing that emerge from engaging and responding to the differences between white and black women. Even though white women may be positioned as social outsiders to varying degrees (in terms of sexuality, gender, and class), they are nonetheless enmeshed in racialized hierarchies of credibility that shape their vision and experience.

If hooks's and Collins's work suggests that Woolf's account of outsider status is insufficiently attentive to racial hierarchy, Audre Lorde's work casts doubt more generally on the idea that exclusion on its own can generate a capacity for truth-telling. For Lorde, exclusion is insufficient to produce a capacity for outsider truth-telling because (contra Woolf) social hierarchies of credibility structure the vision even of the marginalized. Racist, patriarchal, and heteronormative institutions educate the marginalized into "tyrannies of silence"[11] that do not simply *silence* the oppressed but also deny them their own language for describing their reality, through teaching them to speak in the language of the oppressor, to adopt and make their own the strategic, patriarchal reasoning that Woolf identifies with professional truth-tellers.[12] Marginalized individuals cannot un-learn the divisive, diminishing, and oppressive language of racism and patriarchy on their own, because they have been taught to see themselves as in-credible and worthless. There are limits, in other words, to the capacity of individuals, on their own, to speak the truth about their oppression in conditions of deep patriarchy, racism, and heteronormativity.

For outsiders to be able to articulate the nature of their own oppression, and to describe what lives they truly value and desire, Lorde suggests that they must depend on other outsiders. Put differently, the capacity for outsider truth-telling is not, on Lorde's account, an individual attribute created by exclusion, but instead a non-sovereign capacity generated and sustained by conversation and solidarity with other outsiders. Specifically, it is outsider connection, talk, and mutual challenging that allows outsiders to begin to trust, and in turn engage in, their own capacity for truth-telling:[13] "[i]nterdependency between women is the way to a freedom which allows the *I* to *be*, not in order to be used, but in order to be creative" (*SO*, 111). Thus, while Fred Moten and Stefano Harney urge us to look for "fugitive publics" that are already there and need only to be "conserved,"[14] Lorde suggests that the deep influence of oppressive language and thinking on marginalized groups means that outsider truth-telling may need to be *begun*, and begun again and again— through deepening existing connections or making new ones, risky dialogue, and valuing dependence between outsiders.[15] Such practices create a space in which outsiders can vindicate each other's speech and teach each other to trust their own perceptions. As Lori Marso puts it in a discussion of the political dimensions of feminist friendship, the "singularity of experience is made possible only by freedom in the encounter."[16]

Lorde describes this creative dialectic and truth-telling between outsiders as the practice of *poetry*: "[i]n the forefront of our move toward change, *there is only poetry to hint at possibility made real.* Our poems formulate the implications of ourselves, what we feel within and dare make real (or bring action into accordance with), our fears, our hopes, our most cherished terrors" (my emphasis, *SO*, 38–39). Lorde is talking here about poetry not as a form of perfecting an arrangement of words, but as a practice of creating a new space where outsiders might be better able to speak and be heard: what she calls "sanctuaries and spawning grounds for the most radical and daring of ideas" and "a language" where feelings "can be shared" (*SO*, 37). Lorde is emphasizing the *poesis* implicit in outsider truth-telling: that it demands and consists in the creation of a new outsider language and space where it can be enacted and rendered meaningful. Far from being an abstruse art form of elites, poetry is the everyday collaborative language of outsiders trying to figure out how they can describe a reality that has been denied and dismissed by elites. Here, the effort to "speak those truths for which I am still seeking" allows Lorde to make "contact with other women while we examined the words to fit a world in which we all believed, bridging our differences" (*SO*, 41). Like Stephen Dillon's "fugitive," Lorde's outsider truth-tellers can, through *poesis*, "name what others could not even see."[17]

Yet even as Lorde argues that connections between outsiders allow them to cultivate their capacity for truth-telling, she also highlights that their societies have taught them to fear precisely this connection. Lorde says: "In the cause of silence, each of us draws the face of her own fear—fear of contempt, of censure, or some judgment, or recognition, of challenge, of annihilation. But most of all, I think, we fear the visibility without which we cannot truly live" (*SO*, 42). This fear of visibility is debilitating not only because it keeps outsiders (especially black women) second-class citizens, whose reality and needs are kept in the dark, out of public view. It is also debilitating because to be afraid of visibility is to be afraid of the meaningful connections with other people that outsiders can forge only through rendering themselves vulnerable to others' apprehension of who they are.

For Lorde, this fear of vulnerability is negotiated (never overcome) not through moral certainty or political institutions, but instead through *pleasure*. If their societies teach outsiders that they were "never meant to survive" (*SO*, 42)—and thus simply seek survival as mere existence—outsider connection generates a fuller, and more vibrant sense of survival, of what Bonnie Honig calls the "more life" that makes "mere life" possible and desirable.[18] Lorde says: "Those of us who stand outside the circle of this society's definition of acceptable women; those of us who have been forged in the crucibles of difference—those of us who are poor, who are lesbians, who are Black, who are older—know that *survival is not an academic skill*. It is learning how to stand alone, unpopular and sometimes reviled, and how to make common cause with those others identified as outside the structures in order to define and seek a world in which we can all flourish" (*SO*, 112). While standing alone may be necessary to outsider survival, it is not sufficient for outsider survival as a form of flourishing. Rather, it is through connections with others that outsiders open the possibility of outsider truth-telling and, at the same time, pleasure and flourishing. For Lorde, "begin[ning] to speak the impossible—or what has always seemed like the impossible—to one another" depends on "stand[ing] toe to toe inside that rigorous loving" (*SO*, 175).[19]

Through telling the truth, outsiders thus open up new spaces of significance, meaning, pleasure, and flourishing for themselves, but they also affirm and reveal to others (through that very practice) the reality of other possible worlds and ways of living. Woolf focuses heavily on this characteristic of outsider truth-telling. Toward the end of *Three Guineas*, she asks:

> Is it not possible that if we knew the truth about war, the glory of war would be scotched and crushed where it lies curled up in the rotten cabbage leaves of our prostituted fact-purveyors; and if we knew the truth about art instead of shuffling and

shambling through the smeared and dejected pages of those who must live by prostituting culture, the enjoyment and practice of art would become so desirable that by comparison the pursuit of war would be a tedious game for elderly dilettantes in search of a mildly sanitary amusement—the tossing of bombs instead of balls over frontiers instead of nets? *In short, if newspapers were written by people whose sole object in writing was to tell the truth about politics and the truth about art we should not believe in war, and we should believe in art.* (my emphasis, *TG*, 115–116)

Woolf is not saying here that if outsiders began to tell the truth, war and patriarchy would stop immediately. Rather, she is saying that if outsiders started telling the truth, at least the possibility of a world without war, and a world on behalf of art, becomes visible. In the context of Britain in 1938, Woolf's act of writing and publishing *Three Guineas* does precisely that. Interrupting the dominant (almost unquestioned) narrative that war with Germany is an inevitability, and that this war is necessary and justified, Woolf suggests that *all* war is complicit in patriarchy and oppression, and that while it may be inevitable, it will not bring full freedom or equality, but rather will further instantiate forms of inequality, unfreedom, and injustice. Woolf creates an alternative to the horizons of a just victory or capitulation to fascism: a future in which we do not believe in war, but in art.

Lorde's work, along with hooks's and Collins's, casts Woolf's vision into relief, showing the white women writers Woolf alludes to as carriers of (and not just outsiders to) patriarchy and militarism. Yet Lorde's appeal to poetry, and her description of diverse outsiders creating poetry through their discussions, is in conversation with, and not just opposition to, Woolf's vision. If Woolf imagines individual outsiders inaugurating a collective future in which we do not believe in war, but in art, Lorde reveals through her writing and practice that this future is already a collective outsider present created through truth-telling – a present that opens a future possibility for all of us, in which we do not believe in racist, patriarchal capitalism, but in poetry and love.

Outsider status here is not an identity but a non-sovereign, always incomplete *capacity* that is activated through *practice*: a practice of, first, telling the truth to and with other outsiders about the connected oppressions of the public and private realms; and second, a practice of *survival*, of truth-telling as a practice of pleasure that endows outsiders' speech and writing with a meaningfulness denied by their societies. Outsider truth-telling is crucial for outsiders, but it also reveals to their broader societies alternative possibilities for how truth-telling might create and sustain collectivity, not as a tool for stabilizing patriarchal war societies, but instead as a creator and sustainer of art, poetry, and love.

OUTSIDER DILEMMAS, OUTSIDER SPACES

Even if outsider status is not fully in the control of the individuals who practice outsider truth-telling, outsiders consistently frame that status and the capacity for truth-telling it engenders as valuable and significant, as something worth defending and nurturing. Yet that status is tenuous. Especially when outsiders begin telling the truth, they become vulnerable to absorption into the public and private realms to which they speak.

In 1892, Anna Julia Cooper published *The Voice of the South*, in which she articulated the unique burden and vantage point possessed by black women who experienced oppression by virtue of both their gender and race. But Cooper did not write *The Voice of the South* only to alert the reader to the unique form of subjection experienced by black women. Writing more than forty years before Woolf, Cooper argues that their forced exclusion from the realm of pragmatic politics gave black women a more impartial and far-reaching perspective that could—if properly cultivated—turn into a compelling, semi-public *voice*. Cooper suggests that this "little Voice"—the voice of the "open-eyed but hitherto voiceless Black Woman of America"—is necessary for a "fair trial and ungarbled evidence" on the question of race. Yet she also says that in the "muffled chord" of the American conflict over race, "[t]he one mute and voiceless note has been the *sadly expectant* Black Woman."[20] By emphasizing that black women's voicelessness nonetheless occupies a presence—even in its muteness, it sounds a "note"—Cooper does not mean to say, I think, that black women can make a sound by being literally silent. Rather, she is suggesting that they make a sound by speaking in a way currently un-hearable by their society. Their social muteness may actually be an outsider volubility.

Yet if this voice must become *more* hearable by American society, Cooper also emphasizes the dangers of becoming *too* hearable, of becoming fully absorbed in the public realm. Absorption is dangerous for Cooper because participation in the public realm dampens and distorts the broad concern with freedom, equality, and truth characteristic of the oppressed. Cooper argues that Black men have failed to sufficiently address the situation of Black women, and also failed to think in a far-sighted manner about race issues, because they are too involved in pragmatic politics: "they [Black men] do not yet see these questions in their right perspective, being absorbed in the immediate needs of their own political complications."[21] Their very practice of politics, Cooper says, may work to diminish their ability to make critical judgments about what they are doing: "American politics, is hardly a school for great minds. Sharpening rather than deepening, it develops the faculty of taking advantage of present emergencies rather than the insight to distinguish between the true and the false, the lasting and the ephemeral advantage."[22] Participation in the public realm, Cooper suggests, sharpens partisan interests, cultivates an instinct for exclusivity, and forecloses deep and far-sighted thinking.

Thus, while Cooper herself enters into the public realm by writing *A Voice from the South* and argues that Black women should cultivate and develop their unique voice, she also suggests that entering into that public realm may threaten their achieved perspective. She articulates the position of the Black woman outsider as a predicament: as a position of subjugation that demands the development of a distinctive voice to both understand and address their condition, but also as a position of (in Brittney Cooper's words) *possibility* that is threatened if they enter fully into pragmatic politics.[23]

Anna Julia Cooper negotiates and does not just describe this predicament when she frames Black women as occupying a unique *space*. She suggests that Black women occupy a "peculiar coigne of vantage as a quiet observer, *to whisper just the needed suggestion or the almost forgotten truth.*"[24] Framing Black women as standing in a corner—and cornerstone (the "coigne")—of the public realm as an observer, Cooper offers a way to think of Black women as able to be in, but not *of,* the public realm. She whispers the "almost forgotten truth" in order to make it heard, but in sounding it as a whisper, she keeps herself from being absorbed into the public conversation. Cooper's figuration invites us to think of the public realm not as a flat or even space, in which all positions are equally hearable or at least *potentially* hearable; nor in which all voices are heard or put forward in equally audible decibels. Instead, her public realm has a complex architecture, with corners and alleys that outsiders can tenuously occupy while refusing to speak and be seen in the terms of louder and more populous locations. Refusing to shout or argue, the outsider whispers, demanding that—if attention is paid at all—attention be given in a different comportment, one sparked by an interruption and *quieting* of the public noise that Cooper suggests actually silences and obscures.

If Cooper portrays the predicament of the Black woman outsider in terms of an *active practice* of standing in a "coigne of vantage" in the public realm and speaking in a whisper, Woolf negotiates the predicament of the outsider by restaging outsider dreaming, thinking, and movement in a space that is connected to, but not absorbed by, the public and private realms: the space of the bridge.

In *Three Guineas*, Woolf continually makes recourse to the image of a bridge to describe the position of the daughters of educated men in the 1930s—a bridge, she suggests, that became available for occupation after the achievement of suffrage and access to the professions. She says, for example, that after the professions were unbarred for women,

in imagination perhaps we can see the educated man's daughter, as she issues from the shadow of the private house,

and stands on the bridge which lies between the old world and
the new, and asks, as she twirls the sacred coin in her hand,
"What shall I do with it? What do I see with it?" Through that
light everything she saw looked different—men and women,
cars and churches. (*TG,* 20)

As with Cooper, Woolf's recourse to the bridge suggests that
spaces outside the domestic home are not all the same. If
women want to leave the private realm, they need not immediately be absorbed in politics and the professions, but instead may occupy the bridge.

While we may think of bridges primarily as places defined by their capacity to transport individuals from one
bank of a river to another, Woolf focuses instead on their
use as spaces for *pausing, dreaming,* and opening up new
possibilities. Rather than being absorbed into the strategic
rationality of patriarchal militarism in public and private, a
bridge, Woolf says, is a place where we might "pause" (*TG,*
23) before deciding on a course of action, and "stand . . . by
the hour, dreaming" (73). While the angle of vision offered
by the bridge defamiliarizes patriarchal standards of
value—from that angle, "the world of professional, of public
life, . . . undoubtedly looks queer" (23)—it also opens up unexpected passageways: not between the opposite banks (of
public and private), but between bridges. Woolf says, for example, let us "turn from our station on the bridge across the
Thames to another bridge over another river, this time in
one of the great universities; for both have rivers, and both
have bridges, for us to stand upon. Once more, how strange
it looks, this world of domes and spires, of lecture rooms
and laboratories, from our vantage point!" (30). Woolf's
mysterious suggestion that we can travel from one bridge to

another suggests that outsiders need not ultimately arrive at a destination (the professions, the private realm, the university) but may remain on bridges, in the spaces of pausing and dreaming, even if they look at and speak to the university and the professions. Further, Woolf is suggesting that bridges are themselves not uniform, but are diverse and surprising ("how strange it looks . . . from our vantage point!") and may serve as places of connection between outsiders.

Yet positioned not just between public and private, but also *over* dark rushing water, Woolf's bridge reminds us of the fragile and tenuous position of outsiders: "Had we not better plunge off the bridge into the river; give up the game; declare the whole of human life is a mistake and so end it?" (*TG*, 90). It is materially and psychologically challenging to live within and speak to public and private realms, while also refusing the terms of those realms. The pressure from material want, family, or society may become too much, or the felt marginalization may become unbearable, and the water may appear more compelling than a tenuous position on the bridge. Yet, like Lorde, Woolf suggests—albeit more obliquely—that thinking and dreaming on the bridge can remind outsiders that they have support and sustenance from others who have also occupied this tenuous position: we can look at "the experiments that the dead have made with their lives in the past" which can help us imagine how we might "enter the profession and yet remain civilized human beings; human beings, that is, who wish to prevent war" (91). The bridge is not uniformly positive and is filled with risk. Yet by imagining this riskiness through situating it on the bridge, Woolf offers outsiders a way to imagine their pain as available for repurposing on behalf of pleasure and a place where their dreaming and queer perspective may become the seeds of really living, writing, and finding connection differently.

Portraying outsiders' dilemmas in terms of *spaces* that may be created and traversed but not escaped, Cooper and Woolf frame outsiders' dilemmas as *a way of life*: a practice of speaking to public and private realms while refusing absorption. Outsiders can whisper truths to the public realm or bring their truths to public and private realms while living on imagined or created bridges between them. Cooper and Woolf suggest that diverse outsiders may generate creativity and truth-telling out of oppression and that the gifts of outsider status may be (always tenuously and with risk) defended and nurtured even as oppression may be fought.

INSURGENT TRUTH

The truths that outsiders offer are far from a set of facts that will be self-evident to all listeners. Even if outsiders give documents, photos, and other "evidence" to their audience, the challenges they and their truth pose to the governing truth regime will make them look suspect, questionable. Thus, while part of outsider truth-telling may involve offering facts—self-evident nuggets of experience—to others, it also always involves a staging of outsiders, their truth, and their truth-telling, as significant and meaningful. These stagings are not, or are at least not always or often, one-time interruptive events that suddenly change public perception. To the contrary, every performance of outsider truth-telling is also a rehearsal, where the truth an outsider tells and their way of telling it is both a staging of themselves as a truth-teller that demands a response and at the same time a rehearsal for the next time they or others will (and must) tell the truth, often the same truth, again and again. By describing the truth outsiders tell as *insurgent*, I mean to capture this ongoing, unsettling force of outsider truth-telling: the persistent staging of themselves and their reality as significant both resists attempts by the dominant to ascribe them forever as worthless and insignificant (leaving open the possibility of change) *and* introduces, invites, and incites the possibility of outsider reality mattering on its own terms.

This tendency of outsider performances to become rehearsals, the strange capacity of Cooper's "whisper" to travel long distances, can be described in terms of an outsider practice of *re-narrating* or *re-performing* other outsider acts so as to allow them to remain not fully absorbed in public and private realms and yet also travel a distance within them. For example, Woolf calls for an Outsiders' Society in *Three Guineas*, but argues that in order to not be absorbed into the public realm, this society must be characterized by secrecy and anonymity: "it is essential that the movement should escape the notice even of keen observers and of famous novelists . . . We must still hide what we are doing and thinking even though what we are doing and thinking is for our common cause" (*TG*, 141).[25] However, Woolf herself publicizes some of these "secret" outsider acts as evidence of the actual existence of such a society: "there is a model in being, a model from which the above sketch has been taken, furtively it is true, for the model, far from sitting still to be painted, dodges and disappears" (136). As I will discuss in more detail in chapter 4, Woolf establishes the existence of her Outsiders' Society by examining "experiments" of a "positive kind [that] are coming daily to the surface of the Press" (136): (1) a mayoress stating at a bazaar that she will not "do as much as darn a sock to help in the war" (137); (2) popular women's sports leagues which do not establish trophies and prizes but play "the game for the love of it" (138); and (3) an "experiment in passivity," when the daughters of educated men absent themselves from church (139), thus revealing the church's dependence on them. In these examples, Woolf finds women engaged in critical and creative experiments to prevent war—by which she means that they are challenging public and private imperatives to support the institutions and habits of their war society.

Woolf's re-narrating of these "secret," "anonymous" acts transforms isolated outsider performances—perhaps not even seen as more widely applicable or interesting by those who perform them—into *rehearsals* for further performances, narrations, or stagings of outsider truth-telling in which outsiders' reality is significant, important, and credible. Further, through her display and connection of these practices (another outsider rehearsal), Woolf reveals how a social system that may appear impregnable (especially in 1938) has cracks in it and that those cracks may be inhabited, expanded, and connected. Put differently, she represents reality not as an objective fact that must be acknowledged as such, but as an artistically and politically contested set of experiences that can be fruitfully re-situated and re-narrated to better reveal its precise, messy contours. Woolf, in other words, sets a new scene of reality: not a scene narrated from the perspective of the professional truth-tellers but from the perspective of an outsider living in the cracks of the system. In Woolf's scene, patriarchy and militarism are not inevitable, but rather are in the process of being challenged by a diffuse, alternative form of organization, one that resists institutionalization and emerges from the courage and creativity of diverse individuals in particular circumstances. Through publicizing these "secret" examples, Woolf offers an enabling setting and a set of exemplars for other outsiders. Adrienne Rich captures a similar conception of truth and truth-telling in her short essay "Women and Honor: Some Notes on Lying." In it, Rich describes truth-telling as the development of an "increasing complexity" that depends on connection with others: "The pattern of the carpet is a surface. When we look closely, or when we become weavers, we learn of the tiny multiple threads unseen in the overall pattern, the knots on the underside of the carpet."[26] While looking more closely at the carpet is an individual practice— or at least it can be—learning to *become* weavers is invariably collective, dependent on attention to the skill and art of others. Rich's formulation gestures toward the limits of individual virtuosity (on which Woolf sometimes seems to rely) in nurturing the capacity for outsider truth-telling. "Looking closely" takes us only so far; collaboration with and learning from others—imagining their acts as rehearsals for our own, or rendering ourselves vulnerable to them as rehearsals for becoming vulnerable to ourselves—allows outsiders to tell their truth.

Of course, this collaboration can also feel threatening to outsider status and truth-telling. If outsiders render each other's truths significant, does this credibility threaten their capacity for truth-telling by enmeshing them in desires for status, success, and wealth? This was Woolf's view, even as she saw the importance of an Outsiders' Society. Yet Rich and Lorde (among others) see collaboration and dialogue as opening outsiders to *greater* complexity. For Rich, truth-telling is a practice of contesting simplistic or monolithic depictions of reality and thus depends on honest conversation *between* outsiders, not just an individual "looking closely" at their reality: "This is why the effort to speak honestly is so important. Lies are usually attempts to make everything simpler—for the liar—than it really is, or ought to be."[27] Truth-telling is thus not just a way to reject the simplicity of others, but *also of ourselves*; and the truth we tell is not a contained nugget (a fact), but rather an ongoing project that we develop through experiments of telling it to and with others.

As Cooper, Woolf, Lorde, and Rich all emphasize, the outsider capacity to refuse absorption while also speaking to public and private realms, depends on cultivating ties with other outsiders and creating and imagining spaces in which those ties may be forged. While outsiders' societies may generate some of the same risks to outsider status that dominant public and private realms pose, those risks are unavoidable. Living on the bridge always involves risks of being tempted to go to the shore, or of falling off altogether, while standing in the corner always involves the possibility that one will be *cornered* by one's allies or enemies. Accepting the risks of outsider connection, Lorde demands that outsiders address those risks through more truth-telling: honest conversation and dialogue about how to resist the replication of patriarchy by white feminists. For Lorde, sustaining the capacity for outsider truth-telling demands an ongoing practice of telling the truth to other outsiders. Yet forging connection with other outsiders also creates the *courage*—as Lorde notes—for outsiders to speak in the public realm, *and* to refuse its incentives. Woolf's demand that outsiders, when offered "badges, orders, or degrees," should "fling them back in the giver's face" (*TG*, 97), can only be met if there is an alternative realm of connection—some kind of Outsiders'

Society—in which one's words and being can find meaning in a different way.

Buffeted by risks of connection and isolation on the one hand and by risks of absorption and exclusion on the other, the outsider thus stands in a position of subjugation, but also of possibility. Truth-telling becomes a way to work toward freedom, connection, and significance, *and* to refuse existing institutional prescriptions of what freedom and connection are and social rewards of fame, status, and wealth. In the next chapter, I turn in a fuller way to Chelsea Manning's example. I suggest that she negotiated her outsider's predicament through what I call *transformative truth-telling*: a practice of telling facts that aimed to change the world, so that she might be seen as a proper truth-teller in it.

CHELSEA MANNING

AS TRANSFORMATIVE

TRUTH-TELLER

WHEN CHELSEA MANNING WAS ARRESTED in May 2010, the key piece of evidence tying her to large-scale leaks to Wikileaks was a set of chat logs between Manning and Adrian Lamo—a hacker famous for his infiltration of the *New York Times* website (for which he was arrested and served time)—in which Manning appears to admit to the leaking. Lamo had given the logs to the FBI as well as to a journalist at *Wired* magazine. The journalist released the logs in abbreviated form, holding back on what *Wired* viewed as "personal" parts that did not directly reference Manning's leaking. After intense public speculation about what they were hiding, *Wired* released the full chat logs in July 2011 and revealed that the missing parts of the logs primarily concerned Manning's questions about her gender identity and her struggles with addressing those questions under Don't Ask Don't Tell. *Wired* had chosen to redact those because they saw them as merely personal. Yet in the full logs— which I take as my primary text here[1]—Manning explicitly and consistently links her leaking of government documents with her own struggles with living under Don't Ask Don't Tell and, in particular, with her struggles with her gender identity. For Manning, her struggles with state secrecy were connected with her struggles with the mandated secrecy surrounding her sexual and gender identity.

In this chapter, I examine the connections drawn by Manning between her public leaking and her supposedly private struggles so as to challenge the dominance of the truth-telling model through which Manning's actions are usually seen: that of the whistleblower. The whistleblower (a term coined in the 1970s in the United States) is a figure from within an organization (governmental or corporate), animated by a concern with the public good (not private interest), who reveals truths about corruption or abuses of power on behalf of assuring accountability. This model has productively legitimated forms of truth-telling that aim to expose arbitrariness on behalf of assuring accountability and adherence to rules. However, this model also reifies a distinction between public and private that tends to *de*-legitimate forms of truth-telling that do not fit into dominant norms of publicness.

If the prevalence of the whistleblower model leads us to see Manning's linkages between public and private as damaging to her credibility, I want to suggest that those same linkages mark her as negotiating the dilemmas of an outsider truth-teller. In this chapter, I claim that Manning's insistence on connecting her "private" struggles and public leaking should not be seen as corruptive of the attempt to speak truth, but instead as a practice of what I call transformative truth-telling. While the whistleblower reveals facts hidden by the state or corporation on behalf of returning each organization to its proper concern with the public good, the transformative truth-teller reveals the public/private distinction as an oppressive dyad, displays the change-ability and transformability of those realms in their own example and practice of truth-telling, and seeks a public response distinct from the accountability demanded by the whistleblower: namely, a public affirmation of the leaked facts and documents as significant and, hence, of a world where outsider truth-tellers would be seen as meaningful speakers of truth.[2] I will argue for reading Manning's leaking as an attempt not only to reveal facts, but also to help build a world where she, as a gender nonconforming person, could be seen as a significant speaker of truth. Read as an act of transformative truth-telling, Manning's leaking appears less as a failed attempt to assure governmental accountability and more as a risky (and still active) contribution to a world where outsiders, who are silenced and oppressed in both public and private realms, would find connections and freedom, a world still under construction.

In the following, I first briefly discuss the story of Manning's life, her leaks to Wikileaks, and her subsequent arrest. I then discuss the shortcomings of the whistleblower model for adequately describing Manning's truth-telling. In the third section, I argue for reading Manning's truth-telling not simply as an attempt to reveal facts that were hidden, but as a response to (sometimes violent) techniques of secrecy that constructed her as improperly public and not worthy of being heard. Finally, I argue for reading Manning's truth-telling as transformative—that is, as aimed not primarily at governmental accountability, but at offering truths that might help to create, and be useful to, a world that is still being built. This world-under-construction, I suggest, is a world (in Manning's vision) where outsiders are free to experiment, both in understanding and living their own identity and in how to collaboratively use the truthful information that she (among others) gives them. It is a world where she would appear as a significant, meaningful truth-teller.

THE STORY[3]

Chelsea Manning grew up in a small suburb of Oklahoma City. Raised as a boy, Chelsea often felt like an outsider in a world of boys focused on athletics and the pursuit of girls and spent most of her adolescence on computers and playing video games. She came out to friends as gay when she was thirteen. As an adult, Manning would often share her story, as a hard-luck coming-out narrative, with people upon first meeting them. In the chat logs with Adrian Lamo, for instance, Manning launched into her childhood story soon after their first encounter:

> i was born in central Oklahoma, grew up in a small town called crescent, just north of oklahoma city . . . i was a short (still am), very intelligent (could read at 3 and multiply/divide by 4), very effeminate, and glued to a computer screen at these young ages [MSDOS/Windows 3.1 timeframe] . . . i played SimCity [the original] obsessively . . . an easy target by kindergarten . . . grew up in a highly evangelical town with more church pews than people . . . so, i got pretty messed up at school . . . "girly boy" "teacher's pet", etc. (*MLCL*, 5–6)

Manning's home life was also difficult. Her mother, who was Welsh (Manning's father had met her when posted abroad with the US Army), was lonely and depressed, while Manning's father drank and was verbally abusive. In Manning's words, "home was the same, alcoholic father and mother . . . mother was very nice, but very needy emotion- ally . . . father was very wealthy (lots of nice toys/computer stuff), but abusive" (*MLCL*, 6). Manning's father ultimately left her mother for another woman, and her mother moved back to Wales when Manning was about to start high school. Manning went with her mother, but moved back to Oklahoma (with her father's help) after finishing high school in 2005. She moved out of her father's house not long after this (in 2006) because of conflicts with her father's new wife and bounced around for a while working low paying jobs before landing in a suburb of Washington, DC. There she stayed with her aunt, who offered her a stable home, and attended junior college briefly, but ultimately felt stalled in her progress and decided (with her father's advice) to join the army.

At the same time that she was deciding to join the army, Manning was creating a gay male circle of friends for her- self in the DC area and was also embarking on her first real relationship. In addition, she was making more and more connections in a hacker culture that she admired but was not totally a part of. Her best friend—Danny Clark—*was* a big part of this culture, living as he did in the pika house at MIT (a longstanding home of hackers and hacker culture) and working for Richard Stallman's Free Software Foundation. Through Danny, Manning absorbed some of this culture and extended her interest in and knowledge of Stallman's ideas (to which I will return later). Manning's move into the army stood in obvious tension with these other strains of her life, which affirmed queer equality (the army at the time was still governed by Don't Ask Don't Tell)[4] and an anti-authority, anti-ownership outlook within the Free Software movement and pika house. Manning's tenure with the army reflected this tension and was tempestuous. She was assigned early on to become an intelligence analyst, which took advantage of her computer skills and intelligence. She liked her job, as she told Lamo during their chat sessions, but she continually found herself in clashes with authority figures. She had angry outbursts several times before she was even deployed to Iraq (leading her supervisor to recommend against that deployment—which was ignored). This pattern of behavior continued in Iraq, and she ultimately punched her supervisor in the face (for which Manning was severely disciplined and reduced in rank). In addition to Manning's confrontations with authority figures, she was very lonely. Short of coming out to her fellow soldiers, Manning was not particularly closeted about her sexuality—for instance, she kept a fairy wand on her desk and posted fearlessly on her Facebook page about her sexuality and opposition to Don't Ask Don't Tell—and was penalized for it by being generally ignored or disliked by her fellow soldiers.

As we now know,[5] in early 2010, Manning began leaking vast quantities of data to Wikileaks (after first contacting the *Washington Post* and *New York Times*) when she was in the United States on leave. She first leaked what are now known as the "Afghan War Logs" and the "Iraq War Logs" and went on to send the video footage now known as *Collateral Murder* (which depicted US servicemen shooting apparent civilians from helicopters) and the huge trove of diplomatic cables now known as "Cablegate." After sending all of this information, but before most of it was released, Manning initiated an online chat with Adrian Lamo in May 2010. The impetus for the chat was Manning's increasing emotional desperation following her physical assault on her commanding officer and her subsequent demotion in rank. In those chats, Lamo assured Manning that "I'm a journalist and a minister. You can pick either, and treat this as a confession or an interview (never to be published) & enjoy a modicum of legal protection" (*MLCL*, 3). Manning shared everything with Lamo, who almost immediately turned her in to the FBI. Soon thereafter, Manning was arrested and jailed, and she remained in prison for over one thousand days before her trial began. For a period of time, Manning was confined in conditions that could be classified as torture, including being forced to sleep naked and kept in solitary confinement for extended periods of time.[6] Manning was ultimately found guilty of violating the 1917 Espionage Act and sentenced to thirty-five years in prison—a sentence that, as *New York Times* reporter Charlie Savage notes, is "the longest ever handed down in a case involving a leak of United States government information for the purpose of having the information reported to the public."[7] After her conviction, Manning officially took the name Chelsea and described herself as trans*.[8]

MANNING AS WHISTLEBLOWER?

In a 2013 essay in *The New Republic*, Harvard law professor Yochai Benkler portrays Chelsea Manning as part of the "long-respected tradition" of whistleblowers in the United States.[9] Whistleblowers, on Benkler's account, serve the vital constitutional role of assuring "oversight" of institutions otherwise shrouded in secrecy—for example (and especially), institutions within the arena of national security.

Whistleblowers "offer a pressure valve, constrained by the personal risk whistleblowers take, and fueled by whatever moral courage they can muster."[10] Benkler argues that Manning should be classed within this tradition—of which Ellsberg is on his account the most notable example—not because of the effects of her actions, but because of the moral "motives" revealed in her statement on her guilty plea.

Benkler's emphasis on Manning's moral motives on behalf of "oversight" of government (or private corporations) resonates with broader US scripts about the figure of the "whistleblower," a term coined in the 1970s by Ralph Nader. Nader similarly locates the importance of the whistleblower in assuring oversight of governmental and corporate organizations (Nader compares the structure of organizations to feudalism), which otherwise might go unchecked.[11] Whistleblowing, Nader says, is the "last line of defense ordinary citizens have against the denial of their rights and the destruction of their interests by secretive and powerful institutions."[12] Nader also, like Benkler, emphasizes the importance of individual moral "courage" and care for the public good as the proper motivations of the whistleblower. Whistleblowing, Nader says, depends upon individuals' "professional and individual responsibility," which consists in "placing responsibility to society over that to an illegal or negligent or unjust organizational policy or activity."[13] For Nader—as for Benkler—in other words, the whistleblower serves an important role in society as a safeguard for the public good when it is threatened by private interest pursued under shadow of secrecy.

We can see this whistleblower script echoing throughout the many articles and opinion pieces written not only by Benkler, but by Manning's other defenders.[14] For example,

Glenn Greenwald—a prolific defender of Manning writing for *Salon.com* and *The Guardian*—continually refers to Manning as a "whistleblower" and stresses Manning's morally pure motives. For Greenwald, the Lamo-Manning chat logs show that "the private decided to leak these documents after [s]he became disillusioned with the Iraq war. [S]he described how reading classified documents made [her], for the first time, aware of the breadth of the corruption and violence committed by [her] country and allies . . . When asked by the informant why [s]he did not sell the documents to a foreign government for profit, Manning replied that [s]he wanted the information to be publicly known in order to trigger 'worldwide discussion, debates, and reforms.'"[15] While Manning's biographer, Denver Nicks, claims that Manning may not be a traditional whistleblower simply due to the vast scope of documents she released—unlike the traditional whistleblower, who releases documents targeted at revealing a specific injustice—he nonetheless stresses that "Manning's decision to leak state secrets was clearly made with altruistic motivations."[16]

By portraying Manning as a whistleblower, Manning's defenders reveal an important part of her story. As Benkler, Greenwald, and Nicks argue, the chat logs between Manning and Lamo and Manning's guilty plea statement show that Manning was motivated in part by a concern with the public good. Manning tells Lamo, for example, that she would not have sold her data "because its public data"; "it belongs in the public domain . . . . it should be a public good" (*MLCL*, 37).[17] Yet Manning's chats with Lamo also reveal a narrative of her acts that connects her struggle with state secrecy to her struggle with living under Don't Ask Don't Tell and with her gender identity. In her introduction of herself to Lamo,

Manning identifies herself in terms of these two aspects of her life: "hi . . . how are you? . . . im an army intelligence analyst, deployed to eastern Baghdad, pending discharge for 'adjustment disorder' in lieu of 'gender identity disorder' . . . im sure you're pretty busy . . . if you had unprecedented access to classified networks 14 hours a day 7 days a week for 8+ months, what would you do?" (*MLCL*, 2) For Manning, the thread that ties these two aspects of her life together is clear: mandated secrecy. As she says after referring Lamo to the Wikileaks website (without directly identifying herself yet as the leaker), "living such an opaque life, has forced me never to take transparency, openness, and honesty for granted" (*MLCL*, 4). Manning's negative experiences of having to hide parts of herself under Don't Ask Don't Tell are not separate from her motives for leaking information; rather, they are part of why she feels the need to ensure transparency of military actions.[18]

When Manning's supporters efface these connections between her personal struggles and her leaking of documents, they do so in order to justify her actions as in service of the public good (rather than private interest or revenge). Yet in so doing, they also unintentionally repeat rather than remedy the injury done to Manning by the Don't Ask Don't Tell policy. Their portrayal of her as a whistleblower, and as what Dean Spade and Craig Willse call the "sympathetic gay soldier," constructs her struggles with gender identity as "secrets" that must be kept if she is to serve the public good. This seems to do a specific injustice to Manning. It also, however, blocks from view a story implicit in Manning's self-representation; a story about how supposedly "private" aspects of Manning's motivations to leak documents may themselves have been formed by Manning's public experiences of failing to fit into public norms of gender comportment in the army.

SECRECY

In her chats with Lamo, Manning describes the moments in which she realized that demands for secrecy about her sexuality, as well as about US actions in Iraq, were not necessary and were actually oppressive. Yet Manning's chats show not just that demands for secrecy were oppressive but that what I call *techniques of secrecy* (commands, shaming, harassment, ridicule) actually produced norms of publicity and privacy in which Manning appeared as an improper speaker.[19] In response to this situation of subordination, Manning portrays herself in a position analogous to, but distinct from, Woolf's "bridge" and Cooper's "corner" of the public realm. Specifically, Manning constructs herself as a "ghost" who is visible as improperly public and private, and *invisible* as who she truly is.

In the narrative of her leaking that she offers to Lamo, Manning identifies two key turning points which sparked her desire to tell the truth about herself and governmental actions abroad: first, her failure to fit into the norm of what I call the "docile soldier" and, second, her failure to fit into norms of gender and sexuality. Following Jack Halberstam, I do not assume that such experiences of failure simply reveal a lack of success.[20] Rather, I see Manning's experience of failure as also revealing problems with the disciplinary norms inherent in dominant notions of "success"—here, with dominant notions of who counts as a proper truth-teller. I discuss each turning point, in turn.

In her chats with Lamo, Manning identifies the moment that she began to have doubts about US actions in Iraq (and the secrecy surrounding them). This moment occurred following an incident where the US military supported Iraqi forces in detaining and perhaps torturing individuals who had distributed "anti-Iraqi literature." This happened during the first weeks of Manning's deployment to Iraq (in October or November of 2009). Manning says:

> i think the thing that got me the most . . . *that made me rethink the world more than anything* . . . was watching 15 detainees taken by the Iraqi Federal Police . . . for printing "anti-Iraqi literature" . . . the iraqi federal police wouldn't cooperate with US forces, so i was instructed to investigate the matter, find out who the "bad guys" were, and how significant this was for the FPs [Federal Police] . . . it turned out, they had printed a scholarly critique against PM Maliki . . . i had an interpreter read it for me . . . and when i found out that it was a benign political critique titled "Where did the money go?" and following the corruption trail within the PM's cabinet . . . i immediately took that information and *ran* to the officer to explain what was going on . . . he didn't want to hear any of it . . . *he told me to shut up and explain how we could assist the FPs in finding* *MORE* *detainees* . . . (my emphasis, *MLCL*, 23–24)

The most obvious thing that jumps out at the reader from this story is US hypocrisy: Manning realizes that the United States *says* that it is promoting democracy and free speech, when in reality it is helping the Iraqis restrict free speech and democracy on behalf of stability. However, there is another important part of this story—namely, that Manning is told that the form of speech she exercises here (essentially, whistleblowing) is not properly public. She is told to "shut up" and instead to

"explain" to her commander how she can help further restrict free speech and democracy. It would be a mistake,
though, to read this moment as a simple *silencing* of Manning.
Rather, her commanding officer also commands her to *speak
differently*—to speak in the register of US interests rather than
in terms of right and wrong, true and false. The officer's command is not prohibitive, in other words, but productive: it
disciplines (or attempts to discipline) Manning into a particular form of subjectivity—to construct her as a proper soldier,
whose speech can be properly heard only when she follows
commands and identifies with the national interest.

Manning tells Lamo that, after this moment, "everything started slipping" and that she "saw things differently"
(*MLCL*, 24). In what way did she "see things differently"?
Despite her officer's command to speak differently—to
simply obey orders—that command did not turn Manning
into a fully docile soldier. Instead, it produced a soldier who
saw her public persona—and the public persona all soldiers
were disciplined into adopting—as complicit in governmental wrongs, as itself a corrupt figure. As Manning tells
Lamo, "i had always questioned the [way] things worked,
and investigated to find the truth . . . but that was a point
where I was a *part* of something . . . i was actively involved
in something that i was completely against . . ."; "i was part
of it . . . and completely helpless . . ." (*MLCL*, 24). Manning
was "helpless" to address her own corruption because the
only way she could be heard was *via the public persona* of the
docile soldier—a persona which could not question orders or
her superiors' view of the national interest. The proper public
speech that Manning had been disciplined into adopting had
no language with which she could question or change US
behavior.

At the same time that Manning was struggling with the command to become the docile soldier that she felt to be corrupt, she was realizing her failure to fit into another norm of proper public comportment in the army: conformity to a traditionally masculine gender and hetero-sexuality. Chatting with Lamo in May 2010, she says, "8 months ago [at the beginning of her deployment], if you'd have asked me whether i wanted i would identify as female, i'd say you were crazy . . . that started to slip very quickly, as the stresses continued and piled up . . . " (MLCL, 39). Those stresses included continual mocking and at least low-level harassment. As Manning says in an earlier set of chat logs with Zinnia Jones (a transgender activist and blogger): "being around my platoon for 24 hours a day . . . it took them awhile, but they started figuring me out, making fun of me, mocking me, harassing me, heating up with one or two physical attacks . . . which I fended off just fine, but it was scary."[21]

Just like her commander's demand that Manning speak differently—as a docile soldier—this ongoing harassment, ridicule, and ostracism by her fellow soldiers was not just prohibitive (leading Manning to "hide" her sexuality and non-gender-conformity), but productive. It was not productive, however, in leading Manning to behave in a more "heterosexual" and/or "masculine" manner. Instead, this harassment worked, first, to simply make Manning see herself as her ridiculers did—as improperly gendered, queer, out of place. Manning says to Lamo that her gender identity is "clearly an issue . . . i mean, i don't think its normal for people to spend this much time worrying about *whether they're behaving masculine enough, whether what they're going to say is going to be perceived as 'gay'* . . . not to mention how i feel about the situation . . . for whatever reason, im not comfortable

with myself . . . i mean, i behave and look like a male, but
its not 'me':L" (my emphasis). Second, this harassment made
Manning feel, in her words, like a "ghost" (*MLCL*, 3, 28,
42)—visible (as improperly gendered) and invisible (as who
she feels she is) at the same time. As Manning says, "its just
such a disconnect between myself, and what i know . . . and
what people see" (*MLCL*, 12). What is it that people do not
see about Manning? Manning does not mean that people do
not see her non-conformity to norms of gender and sexuality. Indeed, that is precisely the problem—they see it all too
well and ridicule and shame it. Rather, she seems to mean
that they misunderstand this non-conformity—that they see
it as revealing her unimportance, her triviality. As Manning
puts it, "im way way way too easy to marginalize . . . i don't
like this person that people see . . . no-one knows who i am
inside" (*MLCL*, 26). Just like the norm of the docile soldier led her to feel powerless—unable to speak truly and be
heard—so too with the norms of masculinity and heterosexuality (enforced through harassment and ridicule) that construct Manning as someone who, because she appears queer
and improperly gendered, has nothing important to say and
cannot be heard as a meaningful, proper public speaker.
As Manning says, "ive been so isolated for so long . . . i just
wanted to be nice, and live a normal life . . . but events kept
forcing me to figure out ways to survive . . . smart enough to
know whats going on, but helpless to do anything . . . *no-one
took any notice of me*" (my emphasis, *MLCL*, 10).

Manning's narrative of how she came to feel unheard
and powerless illustrates Michael Warner's claim that some
attributes are coded as unfit to appear in public (especially
non-conforming sexuality and gender identity) not *before* public discourse, but *through* it: for example (and as in

Manning's case), through ridicule, ostracism, harassment, and denial of some of the right to speak.[22] To put the point differently, the disconnect felt by Manning—between who she is and who others see—is not produced by the actual invisibility of her sexuality and gender, but rather by others' construction of that sexuality and gender performance as illicit, deviant, and best kept to herself. This is the "open secret" of sexuality described by Eve Sedgwick—where queer persons' sense of invisibility is actually the product of their *vis*ibility, and their vulnerability to the constructions of their identity by others.[23] The logic of the "open secret" in Manning's case renders her always improperly public insofar as she is always articulated by others as bringing the properly private into the public.

If we were evaluating Manning's acts according to the traditional whistleblower model, her struggles with the secrecy mandated by Don't Ask Don't Tell would appear irrelevant at best and, at worst, as problematic for Manning's attempt to tell the truth about governmental bad acts in Iraq and Afghanistan. In this model, if Manning's personal struggles influenced, or were linked with, her whistleblowing in any way, then the act of truth-telling appears no longer as an act that simply renders facts visible that were being kept hidden—on behalf of the public good—but as a possibly biased attempt to (mis)use facts on behalf of private interest.

Yet Manning's narrative of her experience reveals, as I have suggested, that this public/private division does not denote a pre-political distinction between two spheres, but is actually constructed through public discourse, norms, and experiences. In Manning's narrative, techniques of secrecy (sometimes violent) *produce* our understanding of the proper distinction between public and private, between what can

appear in public and what should be hidden. They also produce *her* experience of herself as a "ghost." Her description
of herself as a ghost is certainly a description of subjugation,
a sense of being less than human. Yet this description also,
I want to suggest, opens onto outsider possibility. Narrated
here to another outsider (Lamo, who discusses his own
sexual and gender nonconformity in the chats), Manning's
self-narration as "ghost" *creates* and does not just describe
an outsider location within a world where, in Lorde's words,
she was "not meant to survive." Manning cannot control her
simultaneous visibility (as improperly public) and invisibility
(as who she "really is"), but her naming of herself a "ghost"
works to render her experience visible as both painful (her
felt insubstantiality and unimportance in public) and powerful: ghosts' spectrality, after all, is what allows them to
haunt the realms in which their existence is suspect. Speaking
to other "ghosts" on the internet, Manning rehearses and
performs truth-telling that reveals how outsiders are ineluctably shaped by the oppressive public/private dyad. Yet this
same truth-telling reworks Manning's embodied (online and
offline) ghostliness as a site of power, pleasure, and connection, rather than pure invisibility.

Manning's chats with Lamo are themselves an example
of her reaching out (as she did to many others, such as the
transgender blogger Zinnia Jones) to render her experience
visible and solicit outsider vindication and connection, even
if Lamo betrayed this outsider appeal in his response. And
in those chats, Manning also frames her own transformation
of her outsider experience via chats, speech, and embodied
comportment, as shaped by other outsider connections.
For example, Manning tells Lamo that she "listened and lip
synced to Lady Gaga's Telephone while exfiltrating possibly

the largest data spillage in American history" (*MLCL*, 37). Here, not only does Manning say that she lip-synced to the music of a female singer while leaking data, she also says that she lip-synced to the music of a singer who herself constantly plays with gender and gender norms. While Manning sees the facts she released as being important to the public good, she also here suggests that there is *more* at stake in her act of leaking: namely, the pleasure she finds in creative, embodied performance of non-conformity to dominant models of publicness. At stake in her truth-telling here is not just the delivery of important facts to the public but the sustenance of outsider pleasure, connection, and world-building—truth-telling, as Lorde describes it, as a way of engendering outsider flourishing.

Read in terms of Manning's lived experience as narrated in the chat logs, the public/private distinction upon which the whistleblower model relies does not appear as a set of criteria that can validate the truth spoken by the truth-teller. Instead, the public/private distinction appears as a disciplinary norm that marginalizes and casts as "inauthentic" would-be truth-tellers who seek to contest techniques of secrecy that classify them as improperly public. Rather than attempting, then, to fit Manning into the mold of the classic whistleblower, what if we read Manning's truth-telling precisely as a response to the techniques of secrecy—the public shaming, ostracism, ridicule, and discipline—that constructed her as an improper soldier and public person, unworthy of notice? Read in this way, we can identify an alternative, and more compelling, interpretation of her claim that she leaked documents on behalf of the public good: not as a failed attempt to serve a public good that excludes her as a proper public speaker but rather as a rehearsal and performance of herself, as a gender nonconforming person and as a person resistant to the army's articulation of the national interest, as a proper speaker of truth and advocate of the public good. I suggest that we call this model of truth-telling transformative truth-telling: a practice of truth-telling that does not simply state facts but that also seeks to transform the world, in part through its own enactment, so that she could appear as a proper truth-teller in it.

Spoken as a "ghost," however, Manning's appeal to the "public good" appears to work both as a defense and unsettling of the idea of the public good. Or put differently, the public good that Manning is advocating is *not* a public good that classifies her as an improper public speaker but the good of a public in which she would appear as a significant speaker—a public in a world that is anticipated (but not completed) by the outsider connections and ties that Manning forged.

TRANSFORMATIVE TRUTH-TELLING

Whistleblowers tend to seek official accountability and a return to the status quo. Manning's transformative truth-telling seeks accountability, but I want to suggest in this section that she imagines her truth-telling in ways that interestingly exceed the terrain of "accountability." In particular, in her chats with Lamo, Manning consistently connects her goal of transition to her goal in leaking national security documents. For example, she says, "i don't know what im going to do now . . . well, wait . . . .obviously . . . i guess i could start electrolysis as soon as im back in the states . . . even before im outprocessed . . . *still gonna be weird watching the world change on the macro scale, while my life changes on the micro"* (my emphasis, *MLCL*, 19). Similarly, Manning says at another point in the chat: "im just kind of drifting now . . . waiting to redeploy to the US, be discharged . . . *and figure out how on earth im going to transition . . . all while witnessing the world freak out as its most intimate secrets are revealed* . . . its such an awkward place to be in, emotionally and psychologically" (my emphasis, *MLCL*, 9–10). What, if anything, ties the two forms of "transition" together? I will suggest that, for Manning, her truth-telling in both cases resists expert control over information on behalf of a more creative, communal, and collaborative use of information.

In her discussion of her hope to transition (from male to female), Manning sometimes portrays her goal as primarily physical—changing her physical appearance to match her inner identity.[24] Yet Manning more often portrays her goal of transition as a more open-ended *practice* of truthfulness with no guaranteed end-point: that is, of experimenting with, discussing, and using information about herself differently. In particular, Manning values the prospect of being able to freely experiment with her self, with who she is, without being monitored by the army: "i just wanted enough time to figure myself out . . . to be myself . . . and not be running around all the time, trying to meet someone else's expectations" (*MLCL*, 9). Manning pursued one such experiment when she came home on leave from Iraq: "i mean, 99.9% of people coming from iraq and afghanistan want to come home, see their families, get drunk, get laid . . . i wanted to try living as a woman, for whatever reason" (*MLCL*, 40). Manning dressed as a woman—"crossdress[ing], full on . . . wig, breastforms, dress, the works . . . i had crossdressed before . . . but i was public . . . for a few days"—and "took the Acela from DC to

Boston . . . whatever compelled me to do that . . . idk . . . but
i wanted to see my then-still-boyfriend . . . i rode the train,
dressed in a business casual outfit" (*MLCL*, 39). Manning
says that she "blended in" (*MLCL*, 39), didn't "think . . . all
the time about how im perceived" (*MLCL*, 40), and "really
enjoyed the trip," with the exception of an encounter with a
transphobic conductor, who loudly said "Thank you, MISTER
Manning . . ." when he clipped Manning's ticket (*MLCL*, 39).
This experiment clearly does not resolve Manning's questions
about her gender identity—she still felt that she needed to
figure things out—but she felt pleasure in her ability, beyond
the reach of the military (even if only momentarily and un-
certainly), to experiment in her self-presentation.

In addition to experimentation with living as a woman,
Manning pursued her goal of transition through talking
about her situation with friends and those she considered
equals (for example, Lamo).[25] In this sense, Manning's approach to her transition is collaborative rather than defer-
ential. Indeed, Manning consistently portrays her desire to
"figure herself out" as standing at odds with experts' attempts
to help her do so. She says, for example, that she is "an awkward patient" for her therapist: "i had an hour session with
my therapist . . . i didnt say word for like 30 minutes . . . i just
sat there, and he took notes . . . im an awkward patient . . . its
difficult to communicate with therapists . . . i try to explain
something, and they twist it around . . . and then they ask
why i dont want to say anything" (*MLCL*, 30). In a similar
vein, she expresses a skeptical view of the Diagnostic and
Statistical Manual of Mental Disorders (DSM) as a way of
categorizing and controlling people: "i don't believe a third
of the DSM-IV-TR" (*MLCL*, 30); "so many Disorders that
so many people fall into . . . it just seems like a method to

categorize a person, medicate them, and make money from prescription medications" (*MLCL*, 31). Manning sees her therapist and the DSM as blockages rather than aids to identifying the truth of herself because, like the officer who commanded her to speak differently in the army, they seem to inscribe her into categories and narratives with which she does not identify—categories and narratives that render her, as in her therapist's office, powerless to speak ("then they ask why i dont want to say anything").

This is not to say that Manning's discussions with friends about her transition—as in the "confession" she offers to Lamo and the coming out story that she tells to people when she meets them—and her experiment with dressing as a woman are not constituted by the expert-driven genre of truth-telling that Foucault discusses in *The History of Sexuality, Volume One* as "the confession."[26] There, Foucault argues that the modern demand that individuals transform their desires into discourse actually constitutes the subjectivity that they believed they were merely confessing. In particular, the modern subject formed by the practice of confession sees her sexual desires, rather than her sexual behavior, as expressing the truth of herself and she believes that she can only dis-cover that truth through endlessly speaking those desires and submitting them to the expertise, and expert categories, of others (the doctor, the psychiatrist, the teacher, etc.). Read through this Foucauldian lens, Manning's resistance to ex-pert definitions does not mean that she is free of power, or of management by expertise. Indeed, her attempt to fully ar-ticulate and speak the truth of herself through the activity of confession suggests that her truth-telling is constructed by a disciplinary technique (confession to experts) that she sees herself as resisting.

However, to see Manning's resistance to experts *solely* through this Foucauldian lens keeps us from attending to the inaugural and productive power of Manning's own narration and interpretation of her experiences.[27] As Jacques Ranciere argues in his depiction of workers' dreams and writings in nineteenth-century France, *Proletarian Nights*, approaches to politics that view people's words as "symptoms of social reality" (Ranciere is worried about Althusserian Marxism) blind us to how those words may also be "*writing and thinking at work on the construction of a different social world.*"[28] That is, even if workers' dreams and writings do not completely escape the world in which they are dominated, these dreams and writings have power nonetheless in creating the living possibility of another, freer social existence. Even if Foucault's analysis productively shows us the techniques of power that are reflected in Manning's act—that is, how her truth-telling may shore up rather than challenge an expert-governed understanding of truth-telling, identity, and sex—we should also ask what reality Manning may be at work in *constructing* in her speech and deeds. What social world does she enact and hope her actions will bring into being? What possibilities might her truth-telling, and the truths she tells, open up that are not captured by the categories and constraints of existing social and political reality?

As we have seen, Manning's depiction of her transition opens up the possibility of, and holds out hope for, a world where she could creatively experiment with the truth of her self, in collaboration with others who are her equals, without being defined and managed by experts. Manning similarly depicts her leaking of government documents as an attempt to subvert expert control over information—a control that renders not just Manning, but the public, powerless to speak about and use it. She says:

> hypothetical question: if you had free reign over classified networks for long periods of time . . . say, 8-9 months . . . and you saw incredible things, awful things . . . *things that belonged in the public domain, and not on some server stored in a dark room in Washington DC* . . . what would you do? . . . *things that would have an impact on 6.7 billion people* . . . say . . . a database of half a million events during the iraq war . . . from 2004 to 2009 . . . with reports, date time groups, lat-lon locations, casualty figures . . .? or 260,000 state department cables from embassies and consulates all over the world, *explaining how the first world exploits the third, in detail, from an internal perspective?* (my emphasis, *MLCL*, 8)

Manning's depiction of state secrecy is not focused here on a particular wrong that has been covered up, but instead on the forms of oppression and control constructed by techniques of secrecy. The state's control over information renders the public subservient to state officials—who claim to possess important information that the public does not—and leaves the public less able to freely form its own opinions and to chart a meaningful political course.[29]

Yet could Manning's truth-telling really challenge the state's control of information and truth? As Cornelia Vismann argues, society's demand for disclosure of files in modern regimes does not challenge the state's authority to record and be arbiter of truth but rather shores up a regime of validity structured by state filing practices—that is, that those practices indicate and constitute truth.[30] As Vismann puts it, "[t]he state compiles records, society demands their disclosure."[31] Through the lens of Vismann's work, Manning's act appears to challenge the state's claim to secrecy while at the same time reinforcing the validity of techniques of filing that enshrine the state as the proper arbiter of truth. In this sense, even if Manning performs truth-telling transformatively—creating space for gender nonconforming individuals to speak truth and act politically—her enactment of truth-telling as a practice of leaking documents recorded and filed by the state seems to render her truth-telling ultimately deferent to the state's authority, or the authority of its file-keepers, to say what is and is not true.

Vismann's work rightly presses us not to overestimate the emancipatory potential of truth-telling, but like Foucault's analysis of "the confession," it may overdetermine how we view Manning's truth-telling and lead us to ignore or be inattentive to the meaning that Manning ascribes to her own actions and to the possible (unexpected or contingent) effects of those actions. To follow Vismann, in other words, might lead us to approach Manning's truth-telling undemocratically—viewing its meaning and effects as *only* pre-determined and constrained by material techniques rather than *also* opening possibilities for revision and transformation through social and political action. How might we understand Manning's truth-telling if we attended to the contingent possibilities that are opened up by her act— possibilities that may not have come to fruition but which may have meaning anyway as rehearsals with other outsiders, forming outsider connections, and generating building blocks for new worlds?[32]

In the chat logs, Manning tells Lamo that she hopes for a public response to her leaking. Specifically, she claims that the point of her leaking is to encourage public discussion and ownership of information that may shift some agency from the state to the public. For example, Manning tells Lamo that "god knows what happens now" once cables are released— "*hopefully worldwide discussion, debates, and reforms*" (my emphasis, *MLCL*, 32). Manning's emphasis here is on the public—albeit an uncertain public—taking up and using the information she released to transform their social world.

Manning's focus on the public is also present when she tells Lamo that the data she leaked to Wikileaks "belongs in the public domain" not only because it is a "public good," but also because "*information should be free*" (my emphasis, *MLCL*, 37)—a phrase derived from the hacker culture in which Manning found a partial home. As Nicks notes, "[i]n quipping 'Information should be free,' [Chelsea] was aligning [her]self with the hackers' free software ideal." The free software ideal is an ideal of collaborative, creative, public freedom in the use of information: an ideal that posits, in Nicks' paraphrase, that "[w]hether it be the source code to a computer program, scientific data, or basic facts about the conduct of a country's foreign policy, information ought to be widely available and exchangeable in the spirit of open, transparent mass collaboration and competition."[33] Specifically, the free software movement, in the words of its guru Richard Stallman (with whose work Manning was familiar), promotes free software "not like free beer" (indeed, "free software" might have a price tag), but "as in freedom." By "freedom," Stallman means the freedom to share the software with others—a freedom that sustains and enhances community, rather than dividing it through creating lines of ownership—and to use it freely, by being able to change it, use it differently, or modify it.[34] The ideal of free software does not suggest that *everything* must be up for grabs,[35] but it does suggest that the "source code" of systems—information about how they function—that affect us and our capacity to act freely and creatively should be freely available, modifiable, and changeable through use.

While Manning does not go into much depth about the free public she imagines, her interest in collaboration, her focus on the importance of public debate (rather than elite accountability), her reference to the importance of freeing information, and her resistance to expert control of information coheres with, and gestures toward, the free software ideal.[36] Indeed, in both her description of her own transition and her hopes for a public transition, Manning depicts truth-telling as part of the practice of building a free community—not only because it assures accountability of leaders, but also and more importantly because it spurs collaborative creativity and experimentation with alternative ways of living, with creating new worlds rather than staying in our current one.

Yet if Manning imagines an experimenting public, her resistance to capturing her own identity (or the identity of the public she imagines responding to her) in therapeutic or official categories also suggests that the public she imagines may stand in tension with the dominant public. Following the work of trans* theorists like Susan Stryker, Paisley Currah, Dean Spade, and Jack Halberstam, I see Manning as imagining a politics of "transitivity" (Halberstam) or what Spade calls a "critical trans politics." In contrast to a trans rights politics that demands inclusion within existing state institutions, these thinkers focus on what Spade calls the basic "unfathomab[ility]" of trans* individuals "to the administrative systems that govern the distribution of life chances": an unfathomability that is both a deep problem because it means that trans* individuals do not receive what they are due, but also a site of possibility as trans* experiences with "housing, education, health care, identity documentation and records, employment, and public facilities"[37] may reveal the importance of seeking to "transform current logics of state, civil society security, and social equality" rather than simply trying to gain inclusion within militaristic, oppressive, patriarchal, and racist institutions.[38] Similarly, Jack Halberstam affirms using the term trans* because the "asterisk holds off the certainty of diagnosis; it keeps at bay any sense of knowing in advance what the meaning of this or that gender variant form may be, and perhaps most importantly, it makes trans* people the author of their own categories."[39] Both Halberstam and Spade argue for thinking trans* in ·terms of transitivity, and *resisting* fixed identity, because fixed identities are susceptible to regulation by an exclusive, racist, patriarchal state.[40] Similarly, Reina Gossett, Eric A. Stanley, and Johanna Burton argue in the introduction to their edited volume, *Trap Door*, that "doors" to acceptance "are always almost 'traps'—accommodating trans bodies, histories, and cultures only insofar as they can be forced to hew to hegemonic modalities."[41]

Manning's resistance to being interpolated into expert and state discourses about her identity signals an alignment with these thinkers of trans* justice, and their call for a trans* justice politics that would resist interpolation into a repressive state, even if that state promises short term gains and recognition. Yet Manning's transformational politics is also the politics of the outsider truth-teller, here, the "ghost": the outsider who does not seek to avoid all doors because they are traps, but rather seeks to find a new way to enter, describe, or even embody the door—so that she might speak the truth to the public, while also resisting absorption into its terms. In this context, we might best understand Manning's appeal to a public as an attempt to turn "*doors* that are always already *traps*" into what Gossett, Stanley, and Burton call "*trapdoors*, those clever contraptions that are not entrances or exits, but secret passageways that take you someplace else, often someplace as yet unknown."[42] On this reading, Manning's appeal to an experimenting, creative public would be to a "trapdoor" public: a public that refuses the terms of public recognition and the constitutive separation of public and private. Manning's appeal to an outsider public that refuses—in its commitment to experimentation, truth-telling, and creativity—the terms of publicity, differentiates her from the whistleblower. The whistleblower surely solicits a public, too. Yet, while the whistleblower focuses on the import of using revealed facts to check private interest and restore the government to a concern with the public good, the transformative truth-teller foregrounds the import of the public refusing its own terms and the terms of the social world it inhabits—a transformation that cannot be controlled (or assured) by the act of truth-telling, itself.[43] While acts of whistleblowing may actually partake of the features of transformative truth-telling I have laid out here, the whistleblower model hides those features from view and portrays the act of truth-telling as constative and conservative, merely restoring the status quo, rather than performative and productive. In contrast, the model of transformative truth-telling I have been developing draws attention to how truth-telling, under certain conditions, may spark—or at least serve as rehearsal for—transformation, not just repetition, of our social and political world.

ANONYMITY

AS OUTSIDER TACTIC

Woolf's "Anon" and Rustin's Quiet Persistence

WHILE WE NOW POSSESS CHAT logs between Adrian Lamo and Chelsea Manning that describe her motives for leaking documents and her decision to do so, Manning initially attempted to leak the documents anonymously. Her data dump via Wikileaks was anonymous, and she did not plan to come forward to claim responsibility for it. In the context of traditional conceptions of truth-telling, this would appear either as a form of cowardice—a refusal to take responsibility for the information she offers the public—or as simply leaving us without criteria to judge the truthfulness and import of the truths she reveals. Yet in the chat logs with Adrian Lamo, Manning explains her decision to leak anonymously differently: as an attempt, as a gender-non-conforming person, to avoid being identified as a *male* leaker.

In this chapter, I explore the possibilities of anonymity conceived as an active comportment or signature of outsider truth-tellers rather than as an *absence* or an attempt to remove oneself from the public realm altogether. I do so by putting Manning's attempted anonymity in the context of other outsider theorizations and practices of anonymity, in particular, Virginia Woolf's discussion of "Anon." as the signature of the woman writer, and Bayard Rustin's decision to remove his name from a Quaker pamphlet he co-authored, entitled *Speak Truth to Power*. I want to suggest that anonymity, conceived as an outsider signature or persona, can work as a politically promising challenge to the demand that the truth-teller be a particular (masculine) kind of person, who lives and speaks in a particular way.

First, however, I discuss the dominant portrayal of anonymity in contemporary debates over whistleblowing, namely, as an attempt to make the individual safe from repercussions, to create a breach in state secrecy while walling off the self. In part through turning to the work of Wendy Hui Kyong Chun, I show why this depiction of anonymity as a problem for democracy is itself problematic. However, I also move beyond Chun's alignment of publicity and freedom in her concept of "public anonymity," in order to conceptualize the promising aspects of anonymity as a practice of *refusing* publicity.

ANONYMOUS LEAKING AND DEMOCRACY

In the age of the internet, we are faced every day with the promise and dangers of anonymous communication. From online trolling and bullying to the anonymous release of revenge porn to Twitter bot accounts, the dangers of anonymity are obvious when it is used to shield individuals from the consequences of harmful, dishonest, and sometimes devastating speech and actions. Yet anonymity can also be a way for individuals to be *more* truthful. This has long been the premise, for example, of face-to-face groups like Alcoholics Anonymous, which assume that it is easier to speak hard or shameful truths if one does not have to take reputational consequences for doing so. And of course, anonymity can cut both ways, as with various actions of the now high-profile hacker group ANONYMOUS[1]—from their leaking of information about the Steubenville rapists to their hacks targeting of the Church of Scientology—and Wikileaks,[2] which published Chelsea Manning's leaked documents but also used the principle of anonymity to shield Russian hackers' acquisition of Democratic National Committee emails from public view.

Within this broader landscape of the risks and political potential of anonymity, I will be focusing here on how anonymity functions in the practice of leaking government documents—a question that, I want to suggest, ultimately offers broader lessons for how to think about anonymity in politics. The question of the legitimacy of this kind of leaking became increasingly high profile during the Obama presidency, as his administration prosecuted more people for unauthorized disclosures than any previous administration. Not just Chelsea Manning and Edward Snowden but government officials who leaked smaller, less explosive pieces of information to journalists, became targets. In the debates around this issue, leakers tend to be depicted as creating a breach in an otherwise secure system of national security. For example, in his book, *Secrets and Leaks*, Rahul Sagar worries that leaking will harm national security and create a tear in the fabric of organizational harmony: "hurt[ing] the efficient functioning of the government, which, like any other collective enterprise, cannot achieve its aims in the absence of loyalty and faithfulness on the part of its members."[3] If leaking threatens governmental functioning, then *anonymous* leaking is particularly "problematic," Sagar argues, because "citizens and lawmakers have little ability to discern [the leaker's] motives, much less to punish a harmful or misguided disclosure."[4] For Sagar, as well as for other thinkers like David Cole[5] and Danielle Allen, anonymity is a problem because facts and documents cannot speak for themselves. Even if leaked documents are obviously *true* (for example, video footage, photos, or authenticated government documents), their truth is not sufficient to justify leaking them. Rather, for these thinkers, we must know whether the leaked documents actually reveal a deep wrong in need of correction, and which could not have been addressed any other way. As Allen puts it, "[b]y cloaking the name of a speaker in silence, anonymous speech puts on the listener the burden of bearing additional investigative costs that a name—and its reputational content—normally reduce."[6]

This portrayal of anonymity as a democratic problem, by Sagar, Cole, and Allen, relies on the assumption that reducing the burden of public judgment by knowing the "reputational content" of an identity is democratically important or useful. Yet as I have shown throughout this book, some identities (white, male, cis-gender) allow individuals to count as proper speakers more than others. In other words, knowing the "reputational content" of an identity may be democratically problematic as well as productive, insofar as naming and revealing oneself allows the speaker to be interpolated into hierarchies of credibility. Sagar and Cole also fail to note that the demand for identity—for the truth-teller to make themselves known—can work as part of a logic of scape-goating that blames leakers for more general conditions of insecurity. Indeed, as the national security state continues to expand to include a huge number of people (many in-dependent contractors) accessing information digitally, "national security" may be less a reality than an animating po-litical imaginary. When Manning leaked documents in 2010, more than 850,000 people had "top secret" clearance[7] (and that number is certainly higher now), and Manning—like many others—accessed Facebook, listened to music (Lady Gaga), and engaged in chats with online friends using the same system on which she was reviewing footage of the mil-itary shooting down civilians in Iraq. As Wendy Hui Kyong Chun argues, the internet and "[n]ew media" work precisely by "erod[ing] the distinction between the revolutionary and the conventional, public and private, work and leisure, fasci-nating and boring, hype and reality, amateur and professional, democracy and trolling."[8] In this context, there is no perfect security, no wall around the person or around the nation that keeps information secure. Rather, Chun suggests that this wall can only be *imagined* through scapegoating individuals for the leaks that are an inevitable part of digital business, cul-ture, and war. And as Chun shows in her work on internet slut shaming, the scapegoats tend to be women, queer people, gender-non-conforming people, and other outsiders.[9]

Viewed in this way, the depiction of anonymity as a problem that prevents the public from making good judgments about security can work as a red herring that distracts the public from a different problem: how the demand for identity helps to sustain hierarchies of credibility and may work as a practice of scapegoating that fuels and maintains a dangerous illusion of "national security." Chun argues for combating this practice of scapegoating by cultivating an atmosphere of what she terms "public anonymity," in which people become freer to say who they are and show their (inevitable) vulnerability without fearing punishment. For example, Chun highlights undocumented activists who turn away from the demand for privacy or secrecy and expose themselves online because "privacy offers no shelter against surveillance and prosecution" and only a fearless publicity will enable them to mitigate their vulnerability (*URS*, 3416). Framing this rejection of privacy as "quintessentially queer" (3416), Chun similarly casts harassed teenager Amanda Todd's "exposure of her name" in her notecard video as a gesture of empowerment: the telling of her name "is exactly the point, for it is a gesture to inhabit this space, to refuse the ruse of privacy and to also assert her claim to be online" (4013). Even after suffering severe harassment online, Todd refused to seek an illusory safety by staying offline, or by hiding her name. Instead, she exposed herself, seeking community and support. While Todd ultimately committed suicide, the imitation notecard videos that followed, Chun says, "reveal that even at the moment in which one feels most alone, one is always with another. This exposure—this repetition—reveals that one is never alone" (4037). Chun is suggesting that the repetition of vulnerability itself—regardless of content—creates community, or at least makes possible a "we" in which individual vulnerability is not demeaned but recognized as part of what it means to communicate.[10] What Chun seems to be after is the anonymity of the democratic crowd, or the way in which being part of a sympathetic crowd appears to allow one a certain freedom to risk oneself, to experiment, and to render oneself vulnerable.

Chun's conceptualization of public anonymity suggests that identifying oneself as vulnerable and marginalized need not feed into the practice of scapegoating. Yet her portrayal of good anonymity as a public practice of risking the self without being attacked coheres in surprising ways with the judgments of people like David Cole who see Chelsea Manning as less trustworthy than Edward Snowden because she did not reveal herself and did not offer a full account of her motives. Even though Chun would likely agree with my critical account of portrayals of Manning as a failed whistleblower, her conception of public anonymity harmonizes with, even as it seeks to unsettle, a traditionally masculine conception of public life, where freedom consists in a public risking of the self. Indeed, read in terms of Chun's argument, Manning appears to have succumbed to the logic of safety that Chun criticizes: that by keeping our identity un-exposed or walled within a gated community, we can control our exposure and protect ourselves from harm. Far from cultivating public anonymity, Manning's would-be anonymity looks more like the anonymity that Sagar and Cole worry about: the anonymity that leaves a disclosure uncontextualized and hence unjustified.

I make this point not to dismiss the practice of public anonymity on behalf of which Chun argues. To the contrary, we should all be able to render ourselves vulnerable in public and not be attacked. Rather, I am suggesting that Chun's conception of anonymity leaves a different form of anonymity—that of *refusing* public exposure—untheorized in ways that render it vulnerable to the kind of criticism and dismissal that Chun herself criticizes.

In the next section, I begin to develop a theory of anonymity as the public comportment of outsider truthtellers: a comportment that allows them to *enter* and *speak* to the public realm, while revealing and refusing the forms of subjugation entering it entails. I do so by turning, first, to Woolf's discussions of "Anon." as the signature of the woman writer and, second, Rustin's decision to remove himself from the list of authors of the Quaker *Speak Truth to Power* pamphlet that he co-authored.

ANONYMITY AS AN OUTSIDER TACTIC

In *A Room of One's Own*, Woolf connects anonymity with the condition of being an outsider: of being unable to appear as a hearable, trust-able, rational person. She says that when "one reads of a witch being dunked, of a woman possessed by devils, of a wise woman selling herbs, or even of a very remarkable man who had a mother" in Shakespeare's day, "then I think we are on the track of a lost novelist, a suppressed poet, of some mute and inglorious Jane Austen, some Emily Brontë who dashed her brains out on the moor or mopped and mowed about the highways crazed with the torture that her gift had put her to. *Indeed, I would venture to guess that Anon, who wrote so many poems without signing them, was often a woman.*"[11] In what sense is this condition of being unhearable (and hence appearing as mad or possessed) linked to anonymity, to the "Anon" who "wrote so many poems without signing them"? Woolf's linkage seems to imply that refusing to sign one's poetry is a way of avoiding ascription as a witch or another marginalized, socially toxic type. Yet to act under the sign of anonymity is also distinct from the anonymity characteristic of silence—that is, of the anonymity *forced* upon women within western modernity. To write anonymously, then, is to refuse silence, but also to write without signing in the terms of public and private; it is a way of avoiding being ascribed as either a witch or an improperly public woman.

The refusal to expose one's name or identity alongside one's writing is also distinct from the taking of a male pseudonym—a strategy pursued by George Eliot and George Sand. These writers, Woolf says, "did homage to the convention, which if not implanted by the other sex was liberally encouraged by them (the chief glory of a woman is not to be talked of, said Pericles, himself a much-talked-of man), that publicity in women is detestable. Anonymity runs in their blood."[12] The distinction Woolf is making is between participation in a system that offers publicity and fame to some (men or those who take a male pseudonym) by silencing others (women) and rendering them invisible, and engaging in a form of writing that resists both the allures and imperatives of that system.

Woolf's discussion of anonymous writing suggests that anonymity may be a way of refusing the subject positions offered to women: witch, wife/daughter, or the mask of public masculinity. Yet Woolf's treatment of anonymous writing does more than simply *describe* the position of anonymity; she also amplifies the possibilities of anonymous writing by naming it *as* a subject position. She does this by giving the woman writing under the sign of anonymity a signature. This woman, and all the other women who have refused identification, are not simply lacunae in history; rather, collectively, they become a figure: "Anon." In other words, rather than depicting their writing in terms of an *absence* of a name, Woolf notes, draws out, and affirms how that absence is also a presence—an identity of refusing to identify. The signature, "Anon," the refusal to name oneself as the dominator or dominated, opens up a discourse or space where one can describe the world as it appears to oneself, where one can speak in and invent modalities and forms that unsettle or stand in tension with dominant norms of speech. This is why Woolf values this anonymity in women: "The truth is, I often like women. I like their unconventionality. I like their subtlety. I like their anonymity."[13]

Indeed, Woolf intimates in a late, unfinished essay that the signature "Anon" offers a way to lampoon and criticize the public/private and male/female binaries that work to dominate women and keep them anonymous in the sense of silent and unheard. "Anon," Woolf says, "used the outsider's privilege to mock the solemn, to comment upon the established."[14] To write as "Anon" is to designate oneself as an outsider, one who does not fit in the norms of public discourse and thus to allow oneself the freedom to say how the world appears to those who are oppressed and marginalized within it. This speech need not be deadly serious but may be humorous and witty, like the writing of Woolf and many of her fellow Bloomsbury writers. Outsider writing and speech, in other words, may be a pleasure.

Woolf thus suggests that anonymity may be both a tactic of oppression *and* an outsider tactic. To be anonymous may be to remain out of sight and thus dominated; but remaining out of sight may also be a tactic whereby one can be at work at creating the unlocate-able space from which one speaks. Through the act of speaking or writing the truth, the outsider resists the world's portrayal of herself as unable to speak truthfully or meaningfully. Yet through refusing to identify herself *as* a particular marginalized individual (or as a pseudonym), the outsider signals that the primary purpose of her speech or writing is not recognition, or at least not public recognition and inclusion within the war society. Rather, she signals that she is interested in a kind of recognition and response distinct from the public recognition and fame accorded to the male speaker and writer. "Anon." is more interested in releasing her truth and her true writing into the world, and creating a (no-)space where truthfulness, experimentation, and art may be recognized and valued, than in being accorded accolades and fame that will simply re-insert her into the dominant norms of the war society.

What kind of space is this no-space? It may be something like the space of an archive, or a counter-archive. While Woolf suggests in *Three Guineas* that outsiders act anonymously, refusing publicity and fame, she also publicizes some of these "secret" outsider acts. Recall (as I mentioned in chapter 2) that Woolf examines three "experiments" of a "positive kind [that] are coming daily to the surface of the Press" (*TG*, 136): 1) a mayoress stating at a bazaar that she will not "do as much as darn a sock to help in the war" (137); 2) popular women's sports leagues which do not establish trophies and prizes, but play "the game for the love of it" (138); and 3) an "experiment in passivity," when the daughters of educated men absent themselves from church (139), thus revealing the church's dependence on them. In these examples, Woolf finds women engaged in critical and creative experiments to prevent war, by which she means that they are challenging public and private imperatives to support the institutions and habits of their war society and also (perhaps) creating new kinds of society. Through bringing these three kinds of acts together, Woolf creates an outsider counter-archive, developing resonances and connections between acts that we might otherwise see as disconnected, and were likely not connected by the participants. This no-space holds out a possible alternative way that outsiders might speak the truth and find an audience, without demanding recognition and publicity in a game that is rigged to favor insiders.

Woolf's outsider counter-archive helps us begin to make sense of Chelsea Manning's attempt at anonymity. In the chat logs, Manning explains the anonymity of her leaking not in terms of fearing punishment but in terms of a reluctance to become a public figure if she is revealed as the source of the documents. She says, "i just . . . don't wish to be a part of it . . . at least not now . . . im not ready . . . I wouldn't mind going to prison for the rest of my life, or being executed so much, if it wasn't for the possibility of having pictures of me . . . plastered all over the world press . . . *as a boy*" (my emphasis, *MLCL*, 9). Manning worries that if she is revealed as the source of the documents, she will be mis-recognized, that she will be read and understood "as a boy." On the one hand, this is a personal worry, a worry that she will become a public figure before she has been able to figure herself and her gender out—and thus that she will be seen as someone she is not, mis-recognized and marginalized as she was in the army. Yet on the other hand, this is a worry about what it means to be a public figure in general, that becoming a public figure means being recognized in a certain way—as a static identity (perhaps Manning will be figuring herself out and changing, in some sense, forever)—and being recognized and judged primarily in terms of (gender) identity rather than in terms of what one says or does. Read in terms of Woolf's counter-archive, Manning's worries appear less as symptomatic of an attempt to withdraw from public life and more as an outsider signature: a new figure of "Anon.," who refuses identification within the war society's terms of publicity/secrecy that Manning was challenging in leaking documents.

Yet it would be a mistake to view outsider anonymity only in terms of its archive: as a signature that marks the limits of public and private forms of identification.[15] In the next section, I turn to a different kind of outsider anonymity in Bayard Rustin's practice of what I call quiet persistence: an embodied style and comportment that refuses the norms of public and private on behalf of pleasure, risky engagement, and community not captured by those norms. If Woolf describes anonymity as a signature that becomes visible in a new, or counter, archive, Rustin's ongoing, embodied refusal to perform public heterosexuality directs us to attend to everyday repertoires of outsider embodiment as practices of anonymity that show the limits and oppressive character of our often un-thought and un-written forms of public and private comportment.

SPEAK TRUTH TO POWER: OUTSIDER ANONYMITY AS QUIET PERSISTENCE

In December 1954, the US civil rights activist, labor organizer, and pacifist Bayard Rustin wrote a letter to a fellow Quaker, Steve Cary, asking that his name be removed from the list of authors of a forthcoming Quaker pamphlet, entitled *Speak Truth to Power*[16] (the first published use of that phrase), that Rustin had a major hand in writing. Rustin's letter came in response to concerns of some fellow Quakers and co-authors, who believed that his homosexuality put the credibility of the pamphlet, and pacifism more generally, at risk. Rustin wrote:

> I am convinced that it [my name] should not be
> listed . . . Among other things I feel that my being listed might

very well lead to some new attack which might gravely delay the time when I can again be useful. On the other hand, if we delay a while yet before my name appears publicly, sufficient time will have passed for making a clear stand. Although I personally, inwardly, feel prepared to make that stand at present, I am aware that there has not been enough time for people with questions in their minds to be convinced.[17]

One way to read Rustin's decision to remove himself as a named author of *Speak Truth to Power* is as complicit in his fellow pacifists' depictions of his homosexuality as a sexual lack of control that must be sacrificed on behalf of the broader movement.[18] Rustin himself sometimes participates in this discourse. For example, in a series of 1944 letters between Rustin and his pacifist mentor, A. J. Muste, Rustin portrays his engagement in homosexual sex while in prison as a conscientious objector (CO)—for which he was disciplined and which disrupted an anti-segregation campaign in the prison—as a result of his "own weakness and stupidity that defeated the immediate campaign and jeopardized immeasurably the causes for which I believe I would be willing to die" (*IMR*, 51) and as a result of being "dedicated to 'ego'" (52), while Muste describes Rustin's homosexuality in terms of "undiscipline," "superficiality," and "arrogance" (76). Rustin agrees with Muste that he must "center upon clarifying the 'springs within'" (51) and "overcoming self-love" through a "discipline" (52).[19] Read in terms of this kind of discourse, Rustin's decision to remove himself as a co-author of *Speak Truth to Power* could be read as Rustin agreeing to discipline his body on behalf of broader Quaker goals of peace and as part of a project of working on the self toward greater integrity.[20]

Yet I read Rustin's letter removing himself as a named author of *Speak Truth to Power* differently: not as part of the

Quaker practice of disciplining the body's desires on behalf of the integrity of the soul but instead as a written marker of a broader, embodied refusal to mask his desires, pleasures, and relationships for the sake of public recognition, success, or status. Indeed, his decision to remain anonymous as an author in this instance is of a piece with his broader unwillingness to separate his homosexuality from his political work. Rather than perform heterosexuality or lie about his desires, Rustin consistently sacrificed status in the civil rights and pacifist movements: leaving Montgomery during the bus boycott due to concern over rumors about his sexuality; resigning from his position in a pacifist organization over an arrest for homosexuality; and leaving Dr. King's organization after Adam Clayton Powell threatened to spread rumors that King and Rustin were romantically linked.[21] Rustin's biographer and a recent documentary about Rustin (*Brother Outsider*) portray Rustin's lesser status in the civil rights movement as a tragedy produced by homophobia— and D'Emilio sometimes suggests that Rustin's lesser status was due to his personal failure to adequately hide or discipline his sexuality to better conform with social norms.[22] I read Rustin's practice of living his sexuality and politics truthfully with lesser status differently: as a non-private and meaningful practice of refusing to give up this pleasure for the sake of greater public acclaim.

Returning to Rustin's decision to remain anonymous as an author of *Speak Truth to Power*, I want to suggest that this written declaration (which we can add to the archive of "Anon.") is itself made possible by his embodied practice of what I will call (drawing on Kevin Quashie's conception of "quiet") "quiet persistence." Even though Rustin signals his withdrawal as a named author of the pamphlet in a written letter, I am interested in how our understanding of this written text changes in light of a longer, lived practice of refusing to separate his public and private life and of refusing to give up having homosexual sex and relationships. This practice of quiet persistence is not easily captured in archival form, but I find traces of it in that archive, and in descriptions by his biographer and contemporaries of his comportment and actions.

While we cannot be certain how many people in Rustin's professional life at the Fellowship of Reconciliation (FOR), a militant pacifist organization headed by Muste, knew about his sexuality, John D'Emilio (Rustin's biographer) tells us that "at least by the fall of 1943, two years after he began working at FOR, Rustin's homosexuality entered the Christian peace movement in the form of Davis Platt, his lover."[23] Platt and Rustin both worked for FOR, and it was clear to his co-workers that they had a special relationship. In a later interview, Platt says, "I never had any sense at all that Bayard felt any shame or guilt about his homosexuality. And that was rare in those days. Rare."[24] Characterizing Rustin as someone who showed that you could have "integrity and be gay," Platt's comments suggest that while Rustin did not announce his sexuality, he also did not seek to hide it; he lived his sexuality honestly, as an integral part of himself. Similarly, D'Emilio notes, "Rustin did not pretend to be heterosexual. He did not lie about his intimacies. He simply chose not to tell." While Rustin did try "to avoid 'public declaration,'" as he put it in dinner conversation with a younger gay man, Scotty McReynolds, he quietly persisted in living his political commitments *and* his sexuality.[25]

Read in terms of his persistence in refusing to give up homosexual relationships, we can read Rustin's CO prison letters to and from Muste differently. While Rustin tells Muste in a letter from this period that he has "really been dedicated to 'ego,'" and that he is now able "to see [his] own guilt clearly, and to center upon clarifying the 'springs within,'" he does not link his homosexuality directly to this problem of "ego," as Muste does. While we *could* read Rustin as agreeing with Muste's diagnosis of homosexuality as a form of egotism, it is also possible to read Rustin as *interrogating* or *reworking* the terms of self-sacrifice. Even if Rustin is worried about his egotism, he may be questioning whether egotism consists in his pursuit of sex with men or instead in the desire for public recognition which demands that he give up sex with men. Indeed, at the same time that Rustin was discussing his problem of self-love in letters to Muste, Rustin also wrote letters to his lover Davis Platt telling him that he did not plan to give him up[26] and asked Platt to share his letters with Muste and another close Quaker friend (Doris Grotewohl). D'Emilio says that this sharing of letters suggests "that [Rustin] conceived his struggle not as a solitary one, or even a private reckoning between two lovers, but as part of the business of a Gandhian movement in America."[27] Perhaps. Yet it may also indicate Rustin's refusal to fully conform to Muste's view of his homosexuality by inserting a different image of it into their conversation: showing Muste that he is committed to disciplining his self-love *and* to continuing to have intimate relationships with men.

We can find traces of a similar, subtle refusal by Rustin to frame his homosexuality as a form of self-love in a letter from AFSC staffer Jim Bristol following a later arrest in Pasadena for "lewd vagrancy."[28] Bristol sees Rustin's "glib and facile . . . analysis of his own difficulty and steps that should be taken" as indicative of "the problem that exists for

Bayard of egotism and arrogance" (*IMR*, 153). While Bristol did not want "Bayard to be abject or to be confused or uncertain," he also thought that he "had not moved too far in this respect." Bristol likely saw Rustin's glibness negatively because he thought it reflected a lack of humility or acknowledgment of having made a mistake. Yet might that glibness also reflect a *refusal* to behave as if having sex with men was wrong, as if his sexuality—and not social prejudice and political oppression—was the problem? In other words, perhaps Rustin's glibness reflects an aspect of his activist life that is evident more generally in his honesty about his continued relationships with men (despite ongoing professional, personal, and public consequences): namely, his persistent refusal to live as if his sexuality were something he has to hide, lie about, or diminish.

Focusing on what Rustin *performs* and *does*, but does not exactly say—and thus does not leave in the archive signed "Anon."—reveals a form of outsider anonymity, or refusal of public identity, that is present in a *practice* or *routine* that exceeds even as it informs the content of his speech. I see Rustin's quiet persistence as a form of outsider anonymity because it is a practice that is not capture-able by public and private norms that designated homosexual masculinity as improperly public *and* improperly private. Yet this does not mean Rustin's comportment was not noticeable and even sometimes flamboyant and queer: Rustin brought his boyfriends to his pacifist workplace during McCarthyism; he engaged in public sex with men; he had sex with men in prison; he flirted with men at parties. He also was an excellent singer, a natty dresser, and he loved to recite classical verse. Rustin's embodied comportment refused the terms of the recognizable, public image of resistance upon which the Quakers continually drew (and which their actions also helped to form): the image of the moral resister to public injustice (Socrates, Jesus, Gandhi)[29] whose truthfulness is testified to by their willingness to discipline and sacrifice their private and bodily desires. The form of self-sacrifice underlying the credibility of this image encourages valuable forms of resistance (including Rustin's own resistance to militarism and racial segregation) but can also be mobilized to sustain the politics of social division and violence: in this case, demanding that Rustin hide and sacrifice his sexuality on behalf of peace.[30] By arguing that Rustin's refusal to conform to this model of public self-sacrifice is a form of outsider anonymity, I mean to indicate that his quiet persistence in openly living his pleasures and politics together refused the terms of public recognition and intelligibility as a moral, non-violent resister.

In contrast to the Quaker moral resister who sacrifices their private self in public, and in contrast to Woolf's "Anon." (who signs, and submits to the public, their refusal to appear in public), Rustin's sacrifice of public recognition was for the most part not performed as an explicitly public act. Put differently, Rustin's sacrifice was quiet. This quietness might appear as a form of complicity in the injustice done to him by his fellow Quakers, a silence about injustice that sanctions the Quakers' portrayal of homosexuality as a burden and risk to their movement. Yet quietness is not silence. While silence, as Kevin Quashie notes, connotes "the absence of sound or movement," quiet can be understood as a "manner of expression"—an "expressiveness" that is "not concerned with publicness, but instead is the expressiveness of the interior."[31] In Rustin's case, his quiet persistence includes his letter to his fellow *Speak Truth to Power* authors and his refusal to capitulate in their narration of his sexuality, but it also includes sexual, romantic, and perhaps bawdy habits, relationships, and practices. Rustin's "quiet" was, in other words, sometimes raunchy and queer, and not just solemn and dignified, and Rustin's embodied sexuality, and not just his discourse *about* that sexuality and his political persona, is an important part of his quiet persistence.

Quashie theorizes quiet as a way to complicate our understanding of Blackness, and especially of Black expressiveness.[32] While, on Quashie's account, we tend to think of Black expressiveness in terms of the subjectivity of public resistance, Quashie argues that this obscures other forms of human expressiveness that reveal the limits of the terms of public recognition. Indeed, to understand Black subjectivity solely in terms of public resistance to racism may create new dangers: of "having one's whole selfhood shaped— hardened—by the imperative of resisting ignorance and insults."[33] Even when "embraced as sites of resistance,"[34] public identity categories of gender, race, and sexuality can "undermine one's humanity" insofar as they reduce individuals *to* those identities. Quiet is a way of talking about a public form of expressiveness—forms of pleasure, meaning, and pain— that shows the limits of public categories and identities, and gestures beyond them to what they cannot capture.[35]

Quashie's theory of "quiet" illuminates the significance of a repertoire of outsider anonymity that refuses to sign itself in public. Rustin's quiet persistence, and his sacrifice of public recognition, calls attention to how one dominant model of Left resistance—the disciplined truth-teller who sacrifices the private self on behalf of something higher— may silence, marginalize, and render illegible certain forms of human expression and diversity, while also serving as a site for their emergence. For Quashie, this quiet expresses an "ineffable integrity" of self that is a "stay against the social world."[36] Quiet signals, in other words, the sovereignty of an individual's internal world even in a political world that calls an individual to be recognizable in its terms.

Quashie's separation of the quiet interior from the public exterior is valuable in revealing the narrowness of public categories for capturing diverse forms of human expressiveness—a point that resonates with outsider concerns. Yet this separation enacts a different kind of closure in insisting that the meaningfulness of quiet comes only in its *opposition* to norms of public recognition. Certainly, the *quiet* dimension of Rustin's quiet persistence expresses his humanity and exceeds public categories of recognition, but the *persistence* of his quietness marks how the practice of sacrificing public recognition may itself, through dogged iteration in the face of dismissal and criticism, become a political model, staging, scenario, or repertoire available both to Rustin and other outsiders. His quiet persistence continues and repeats, working as a rehearsal for him and others, in directions that neither Rustin nor we can anticipate. In particular, in his everyday refusal to separate his sexuality from social connections and political action, Rustin's queer quietness works at creating an atmosphere where new forms of connection and recognition become possible or at creating what Patchen Markell calls "contexts" that enable "responsiveness" to new forms of political action.[37]

In Rustin's discussion of his participation in the Journey of Reconciliation (riding in the "white" sections of buses in the US South in the 1940s), Rustin described his and other activists' early persistence on civil rights issues in these terms: as creating an atmosphere that allowed the civil rights struggles of the late 1950s to gain public attention and traction. Rustin says, "[w]ithout that constant experimentation, 'I . . . do not believe Montgomery would have been possible nor successful except for . . . the long experience people had about reading about sitting in buses and getting arrested, so that people have become used to hearing this'" (*IMR*, 144). Similarly, we might view Rustin's persistent sacrifice of public recognition and fame, his refusal to separate his sexuality from his politics, as being at work at creating a world where lives such as his could find future significance. Here, Rustin's quiet persistence does not offer a public challenge to homophobia and its politics of persecution but instead works at creating settings and scenes where resistance to that politics becomes more possible.

ANONYMITY: ARCHIVE AND REPERTOIRE

If we read Manning's anonymity as a Woolf-ian signature (Anon.), we can affirm her refusal to name herself as the leaker of documents as an expression of a claim that norms of public recognition could not capture her experience, identity, and action. Read in this way, her leaking of documents appears as a kind of writing or speech that could have (if she had remained anonymous) called us to imagine and imitate a more experimental and open-ended form of writing and speaking truth. Yet Manning's distinctive signature came into view only because Adrian Lamo, whom she had approached via a private chat, leaked to the FBI the chats in which she appeared to admit to leaking documents. Lamo, who heard Manning's privately expressed worries about having her picture plastered all over the world "as a boy," ensured that this would happen. Of course, as Chun says, this leakiness is part of what the internet is, and is also valued by Manning. The blurring of public and private can be both emancipatory and disciplinary/oppressive. While we could respond to Lamo's "outing" of Manning in Chun's terms— by fighting for the right to be vulnerable in public without being attacked—I would like to position Lamo's leaking (of Manning's leakiness) differently here: as a terrible personal betrayal with devastating consequences that also, and at the same time, renders Manning's example, thinking, and speech available to us, as a position in a network of outsider speech and action.

Yet Manning's anonymity would have been valuable even if the public were not broadly aware that she sought anonymity because she did not want her picture plastered all over the world "as a boy." Manning's persistent anonymous signature (she leaked documents multiple times to Wikileaks) could have served as a rehearsal for other outsiders, communicated and revealed through oblique and partial channels, like on-line chats. In addition, Manning's repertoire of anonymity— her quiet persistence in refusing to separate her sexuality and gender non-conformity from her work in the army (putting a fairy wand on her desk, for example), her practice of reaching out to other outsiders while still in the army, her refusal to hide her queer sexual and romantic relationships— was an embodied model for other outsiders and helped to create connections between them.

Reconceiving anonymity as an outsider signature, as well as an embodied repertoire of refusing public and private norms, I have suggested that anonymity is a promising tool of outsider truth-telling. I make this argument not to suggest that we can fully disentangle these promising practices of anonymity from the damaging practices of anonymous bullying, trolling, and propagandizing. Rather, I mean to broaden the geography of anonymity to include not just the hiding of identifying markers as a way of avoiding consequences for bad acts but also the refusal of public and private norms; not just a denial of authorship, but an embodied style that resists conformity to public and private norms of comportment. Conceived in this way, anonymity appears less as a withdrawal of the self from the public realm and more as a contested, diverse, and risky style of engagement *with* the public realm, a style of refusing its terms not through silence, but through pleasurable and risky writing, through singing, having sex, talking, comporting oneself, and through entangling oneself with others. If we view anonymity as a capacious and contested form of engagement with the public realm, anonymity may not *only* call us to demand identification; it may also call us to ask how the public and private realms may need to change so that everyone can appear in them as a significant, meaningful speaker. Anonymity may not call us, in other words, to demand the unmasking of the speaker but instead call us to change the world so that outsider speakers, writers, or political actors may appear in it as significant.

TELLING THE TRUTH,

CHANGING THE WORLD

Woolf's War Photographs and Manning's Collateral Murder Video

IF MODERN WARFARE IS, AS Paul Virilio argues, essentially cinematic[1]—entwined with techniques of aerial image-ization that render the enemy visible and kill-able—the release to the public of photos and films of the battlefield seems to often resist or push back on the military operationalization of images. Famously, photos of the suffering caused by the US military in Vietnam helped to turn the tide of public opinion against the war. Recently, the photo of a dead Syrian boy on a beach—who drowned while fleeing his war-torn country—helped to awaken public sentiment in favor of welcoming Syrian refugees.

Yet photos of atrocities, suffering, and abuses in war also often cannot fulfill the burden put on them—that is, to offer a truth so obvious, so irrefutable, that it calls for redress. For example, the leaked photos showing the torture and suffering inflicted on military detainees at Abu Ghraib stirred public outrage and debate about US tactics in the so-called

War on Terror. Yet even though many of us, and writers such as Susan Sontag and Mark Danner, saw them as obviously showing systematic torture and abuse in contravention of the Geneva conventions, the photos did not create the unified outrage and check on US abuses that many assumed should follow from their release. Nor did it prompt a change in US tactics or a decisive turn in public opinion against the war. As W. J. T. Mitchell put it: "there has been a longing for the Abu Ghraib images to have a decisive power and effect that has so far eluded them. This desire was especially acute in the immediate aftermath of their unveiling, when it was hoped that the images were the 'smoking gun' that would bring down the government that had produced them."[2] Far from a becoming a smoking gun, the Abu Ghraib images became sites of political contestation over what exactly we were seeing: Some fraternity-esque hijinks? A few "bad apples"? A systematic pattern of abuse and law-breaking? Was the problem to address the leaking of the images, or what the images reveal?[3]

In this chapter, I do not look at the Abu Ghraib photos but instead at Chelsea Manning's release of a different set war images—the raw video and audio footage, recorded from a US Apache helicopter, from a July 2007 incident in a Baghdad suburb (New Baghdad) in which the US military killed twelve people, including two Reuters employees, and badly wounded two children. Rather than reading this footage in terms of a smoking-gun ideal of what images should do—that is, that they should prompt military and governmental reforms—I argue for a different interpretation of Manning's action. Turning to Virginia Woolf's use of war photographs in *Three Guineas*, I argue for reading Manning's release of the footage as an act that begins to change the world by transforming the material settings and props through which we access the world (our devices and the spaces in which we use them): by transforming those devices (phones, TVs, computers, tablets) from their functional assignments (pleasure, intimacy, sociality, commerce, work) into sites of *leaking*, sites where cracks and connections emerge between public and private, war and peace, male and female, and where outsider truths can be told. Truth-telling here is not a way of shoring up law and government from corruptive cracks—fixing the fractures of deception and abuse—but instead a way of both revealing and generating new fissures through which we might speak and see realities thus far obscured. I show one way in which the transformation effected by Manning's leaking had a concrete effect: namely, in prompting Ethan McCord, a soldier who appears in the video footage, to come forward and speak about his experiences in, and disillusion with, the Iraq war.

First, however, I argue for reading Woolf's use of war photographs in *Three Guineas* as a practice of changing the world, through putting her in conversation with Susan Sontag and Judith Butler and their approaches to images of war and suffering.

PUTTING PHOTOGRAPHS ON THE TABLE: OUTSIDER TRUTH-TELLING AND CHANGING THE WORLD

Throughout *Three Guineas*, Woolf appeals to a set of photographs as revealing the truth of war. These photos, sent by the Spanish Government "with patient pertinacity about twice a week," are "not pleasant photographs to look upon" (*TG*, 14). They are, Woolf says, photographs of dead bodies for the most part. This morning's collection contains the photograph of what might be a man's body, or a woman's; it is so mutilated that it might, on the other hand, be the body of a pig. But those certainly are dead children, and that undoubtedly is the section of a house. A bomb has torn open the side; there is still a birdcage hanging in what was presumably the sitting-room, but the rest of the house looks like nothing so much as a bunch of spilikins suspended in mid-air. (14)

Woolf continues to refer back to the photos throughout the book—for example, asking various imagined or real interlocutors to examine the "photographs that are all this time piling up on the table—photographs of more dead bodies, of more ruined houses" (50), or to consider "the photographs of dead bodies and ruined houses that the Spanish government sends almost weekly" (83).

On the one hand, Woolf's ongoing references to the photos throughout the book appear to reflect an appeal to a set of obvious facts that could offer a common ground of judgment that unites men and women, even if their means of action (outsider/insider) to prevent war differs. Indeed, she says as much to her male pacifist interlocutor early on:

[p]hotographs . . . are not arguments addressed to the reason; they are simply statements of fact addressed to the eye . . . When we look at these photographs some fusion takes place within us; however different the education, the traditions behind us, our sensations are the same; and they are violent. You, Sir, call them "horror and disgust." We [women] also call them horror and disgust. (*TG*, 13–14)

This alignment in feeling leads to an alignment in judgment: "the same words rise to our lips. War, you say, is an abomination; a barbarity; war must be stopped at whatever cost. And we echo your words. War is an abomination; a barbarity; war must be stopped" (14). Looking at these photographs, Woolf seems to suggest, leads to unity in feeling and purpose.

This is also how Susan Sontag, who is critical of Woolf, reads her. For Sontag, Woolf has a naïve faith in the power of images to create unity. Sontag's Woolf sees photos as determining the public narrative,[4] while Sontag argues that photos, on their own, are radically *in*determinate. Even if all photos reflect a particular "point of view,"[5] "[p]hotographs of an atrocity may [still] give rise to opposing responses. A call for peace. A cry for revenge. Or simply the bemused awareness, continually restocked by photographic information, that terrible things happen."[6] Because, for militants, "identity is everything," "all photographs wait to be explained or falsified by their captions."[7] For Sontag, the ethical import of photos of war and suffering lies not in their capacity to change public opinion[8] but rather in their capacity to haunt us in a more abstract way: as reminders of "what human beings are capable of doing—may volunteer to do, enthusiastically, self-righteously. Don't forget."[9] Images do not incite us to action, but are "an invitation" for individual critical reflection about how such harms are made possible.[10]

Sontag thus positions Woolf as a naïve foil to her own more "realistic" view of the limited power of images of atrocity. In *Frames of War*, Judith Butler (without discussing Woolf) argues that Sontag underestimates the power of images to change public opinion and spark political action. Butler sees this power, however, less in the transparency of the message of the photographs and more in their capacity to reveal and call us to judge their "frame"—that is, the affective delimitation of a scene as portraying some lives as grievable and others not.[11] For Butler, images of suffering do this through their *circulation* and *temporality*. While photos have to circulate in order to generate affective and sensory consent to war, this circulating means that the photo's frame inevitably breaks apart,[12] creating opportunities for resistance: "[t]he frame, in this sense, permits—even requires—this breaking out. This happened when the photos of Guantanamo prisoners kneeling and shackled were released to the public and outrage ensued; it happened again when the digital images from Abu Ghraib were circulated globally across the internet, facilitating a widespread visceral turn against the war."[13] These photographs, which were manufactured to help sustain both the workings and apparent pleasures of torture and war for their perpetrators, when circulated into the public realm, revealed not just wrongdoing, but the "frame" of war: that the lives of detainees were not seen as grievable, and that our assent to seeing some lives as ungrievable is part of what allows war to happen.

Further, however, Butler argues that the temporality of photos of suffering—that "the photograph acts on us in part through outliving the life it documents," "anticipating and performing that grievability"[14]—means that these images also inherently call us to grieve lives we had previously not felt to be grievable, and through that grievability, to feel the demand to judge these lives equally worthy of care and justice.[15] If Sontag's Woolf sees images of war as powerful insofar as they determine public narratives of war and unite us, Butler sees images of war as powerful because their transmission makes possible, and even demands, new narratives and judgments about war, based in the felt grievability of the lives of those who had previously been deemed ungrievable.

At stake in the debate between Butler and Sontag is *whether* photographs make a political and ethical demand on us that we cannot control. I would like to complicate this debate by complicating Sontag's reading of Woolf and drawing attention to how the question of whether photographs place a political or ethical demand on us may distract us from something else that the act of releasing photos or images may do, and which I see Woolf foregrounding in her use of Spanish Civil War photos: namely, not change *us*, but change the *world* so that truth-telling becomes more possible.

If Sontag sees Woolf as assuming that pictures of suffering create unity, I want to focus on how Woolf purposefully stages a disconnect between the images she claims to be seeing, as the narrator, and the images that *we* (her readers) see. Even as Woolf describes photos of ruined houses and dead children, she does not print copies of these photos in *Three Guineas*. Instead, she prints copies of other photos in the book, which she never appears to actually mention or refer to in the book: five photos of older white British men in diverse professional, church, and military attire. In other words, she seems to discuss and refer back to one set of photos in the text of the book, while actually displaying a different set of photos. Some of her readers argue that Woolf's failure to print the Spanish war photos is a marker of her attempt to call on or create a collective memory of these events or of her sense that writing is more truthful than the photos themselves—which would put her in Sontag's camp.[16] I see the explanation for Woolf's apparent omission of the Spanish war photos differently. I read her discussion of the Spanish war photos in the text of the book not as an appeal to actual images but rather as part of an attempt to change the world in such a way that when we look at the insignia and performance of patriarchy and militarism in the published photos in *Three Guineas*, we also see the suffering and war she describes in the Spanish Civil War photos.

Indeed, at the end of the book, Woolf says that when we look again at the "picture of dead bodies and ruined houses that the Spanish Government sends us almost weekly" (*TG*, 167):

> it is not the same picture that caused us at the beginning of this letter to feel the same emotions—you called them "horror and disgust"; we called them horror and disgust. For as this letter has gone on, adding fact to fact, *another picture has imposed itself upon the foreground*. It is the figure of a man; some say, others deny, that he is Man himself, the quintessence of virility, the perfect type of which all the others are imperfect adumbrations. He is a man certainly. His eyes are glazed; his eyes glare. His body, which is braced in an unnatural position, is tightly cased in a uniform. Upon the breast of that uniform are sewn several medals and other mystic symbols. His hand is upon a sword. He is called in German and Italian Fuhrer or Duce; in our own language Tyrant or Dictator. And behind him lie ruined houses and dead bodies—men, women and children. (my emphasis, 168)

In this new rendering of the photos, the connections between patriarchy and militarism, between the private and public oppressions of women become visible. Woolf is suggesting that the picture of Spanish civil war atrocities has literally *changed*, that it has become a picture of a military man with the ruined houses and dead bodies strewn around him.

The point of being able to see these two things as part of the same picture is twofold for Woolf. First, it reveals, viscerally, the connections between public and private oppression, between militarism and patriarchy: "that the public and the private worlds are inseparable connected; that the tyrannies and servilities of the one are the tyrannies and servilities of the other" (*TG*, 168). Yet the presence of the "human figure even in a photograph suggests other and more complex emotions" for Woolf—namely, that the photo, as Sontag said of the Abu Ghraib photos, is us:[17] "we cannot," Woolf says, "dissociate ourselves from that figure but are ourselves that figure." For Sontag, this indicates our complicity in the culture of war atrocity, as it does also for Woolf. Yet Woolf also sees this complicity as revealing the possibility of change. The presence of the human figure "suggests that we are not passive spectators doomed to unresisting obedience but by our thoughts and actions can ourselves change that figure" (168–169). To see the picture as Woolf argues we have come to see it in the course of the book is not only crucial to revealing our complicity and enmeshment in the suffering of war and the oppressions of public and private; it is also crucial to changing that complicity.

If Sontag sees our ideologies as determining our reception of such photos, and Butler sees photos as possessing a circulatory power to disrupt our narratives, Woolf's discussion of the Spanish Civil War photos suggests that *acts of disclosure*—here, her own act of disclosure in *Three Guineas*—can change how we see photos. In other words, photos appear in Woolf's writing neither as passive recipients of our ideologies, nor (contra Sontag) as active shapers of those ideologies, but as mediated images which can appear in different ways depending on the material circumstances of their disclosure. In the next section, I dig more deeply into *how* Woolf discloses the images to the reader/viewer, and I suggest that in her discussions of tables, Woolf enacts truth-telling as a situated practice that may actually change the material setting in which it happens. This change does not exert a determinative ethical demand on the reader/viewer but rather changes the world in ways that may enable us to better hear the truth-telling of outsiders, those not authorized or sanctioned by existing hierarchies.

Indeterminate Tables

If Woolf's depiction of the bridge offers a situated depiction of the outsider's truthful standpoint, her depiction of "tables" in *Three Guineas* offers a way to think about how outsiders might transform existing spaces into places of truth-telling. If the "table" of facts, figures, and statistics is, as Foucault has argued, a disciplinary tactic of truth-power in the modern era, Woolf makes recourse to another kind of "table" in *Three Guineas* as a necessary prop of truth-telling—the table on which one puts newspapers and letters, around which one dines, and which one shares with diverse people for diverse purposes (politics, a tête-à-tête, meetings, etc.). If Foucault's table, like the numerical columns of double-entry book-keeping, exemplifies one system of representing truth as self-evident, Woolf's table offers an alternative: a way of representing truth that is not a common ground but that *stages a new scene* in which the possibility of acting and speaking differently, and saying different things, arises. The tables of *Three Guineas*, in other words, are objects that move between serving public and private functions but may also become sites of outsider truth-telling.

We all, Woolf says, have our own tables. For example, when Woolf summons in imagination the daughter of an educated man who has enough to live upon, she portrays her as "examin[ing] the products of that reading and writing which lie *upon her own table*" (my emphasis, *TG*, 113). Similarly, Woolf says in her discussion of education that "[t]he honorary treasurer of the Rebuilding Fund" "seemed to say," "'What is the use of thinking how a college can be different,' . . . 'when it must be a place where students taught to obtain appointments?' 'Dream your dreams,' she seemed to add, turning, rather wearily, *to the table which she was arranging for some festival*, 'fire off your rhetoric, but we have to face realities'" (my emphasis, 45). The honorary treasurer of the professional women's organization also has a table. Woolf writes to her, "since, in one word, it is obvious that you are busy, let us be quick; make a rapid survey; discuss a few passages in the books in your library; in the papers *on your table*, and then see if we can make the statement less vague, the conditions [for giving our guinea to the organization] more clear" (my emphasis, 73).

Tables also can be gendered. During Woolf's childhood, women and men did not mix socially, except at formal social gatherings (indeed, when she and her sister, Vanessa, began to socialize with Lytton Strachey, J. M. Keynes, and the other members of what would become known as the Bloomsbury Group, it was a new experience for all of them to talk openly with members of the opposite sex[18]) and, in a footnote, she draws attention to the dining table as a traditional site of masculine speech and discourse, quoting C. E. M. Joad (a prominent pacifist) as saying, "[w]omen, I think, ought not to sit down to table with men; their presence ruins conversation, tending to make it trivial and genteel, or at best merely clever" (*TG*, fn, 188). If women have tables where they dine and organize their letters and their bazaars, men have their own tables, where they dine, organize their papers, and (among other things) plan war.

However, Woolf suggests that the table can also become a place for outsider truth-telling. Indeed, Woolf's first evocation of the Spanish Civil War photos does not happen abstractly; rather, she tells her male pacifist interlocutor that she is going to put the photographs "on the table": "Let us see then whether when we look at the same photographs we feel the same things. *Here then on the table before us are photographs.* The Spanish Government sends them with patient pertinacity about twice a week . . . " (my emphasis, *TG*, 14). Given Woolf's portrayal of tables as the material conditions of the activities of the war society, her depiction of herself as putting the photographs "on the table" works as a critical rejoinder: suggesting that the tables of the war society can be mobilized differently, for truth-telling.

Woolf's depiction of truth-telling as an act of putting the photographs "on the table" also suggests that truth-telling, like the activities of the war society, should not be understood abstractly—neither as an act of pure communication between individuals, nor as a structural logic inherent, as Butler argues, in the "circulation" of photos. Rather, truth-telling requires a particular kind of material setting and support. What kind of setting? In *Three Guineas*, the table on which she sets photographs for her interlocutor to view is not situated in any particular room; we do not know if it is a dining table, a writing table, or a table in a committee room. By calling us to look at the photographs on "the table before us" without ascribing it to any particular locale or purpose, Woolf suggests that the kind of setting required to tell the truth is precisely a setting that is outside of, or which exceeds, curated public and private spaces, which dictate the purpose of the objects therein (that the table is for planning war, or for eating with members of our own sex, or for planning bazaars). If we do not know what the table is *for*, then we cannot assume that we know what the truth laid on that table is for either. Here, Woolf offers a rejoinder to Sontag's point that photos can serve all kinds of ideologies; the photos of "ruined houses and dead bodies" can certainly be seen as justification for war. But what if, Woolf is saying, we put these photos on a table with no pre-ordained purpose, with no ideology or function guiding its use? What, then, do those photographs lead us to think or do? If they are laid on an indeterminate table, the possibilities for action and agency may become open and new. As Woolf says, rejecting any automatic acceptance of the suggestions of her interlocutor, "what active method is open to us?" (*TG*, 15)

Yet tables are always situated. They always are in one room or another, one part of the house or the office. How can a table become indeterminate, a space for telling truths that opens the space for new actions and methods? In *Three Guineas*, the table becomes indeterminate—it sets a new, as yet unwritten scene—precisely when Woolf lays the photographs on it. In other words, if an indeterminate setting, a table that has no pre-given purpose, enables truth-telling, putting our truths *onto* a table lifts that table out of its situated-ness, rendering it a place whose purpose and meaning is no longer determined by its public or private location. This does not mean that putting the photographs on the table creates unity or determines the public narrative about war. Rather, I am suggesting that we should read the "success" of truth-telling, of releasing images of atrocity, in a register distinct from the one Butler and Sontag address (creating unified or transformed public opinion). What Woolf's depiction of putting the photographs on the table suggests is that acts of disclosure may generate a kind of good distinct from public unity or official account-ability: the good of dis-engaging spaces from the tyrannies of public and private and rendering them more available for further truth-telling.

Indeed, as *Three Guineas* goes on, Woolf's courage in speaking the truth appears to grow, and the table becomes more and more laden with the truth she tells, becoming a site of spectacular display of the connections between war's horror and domestic dictatorialness: "Let us then lay your letter asking for help to prevent war, before the inde-pendent, the mature, those who are earning their livings in the professions . . . That surely will be enough without pointing to the photographs that are all this time piling up on the table—photographs of more dead bodies, of more ruined houses to call forth an answer, and an answer that will give you, Sir, the very help that you require" (*TG*, 50–51). She piles other letters next to his on the table, to show that his request for help in preventing war requires contextualization and attenuation vis-à-vis patriarchy: "doubts and hesitations there are; and the way to understand them is to place before you another letter, a letter as genuine as your own, a letter that happens to lie beside it on the table" (51). And in the last chapter, the table is fully transformed into a new stage of truth-telling, displaying the fact of Woolf's refusal to join the male pacifist's society: "Let us then keep the form unsigned on the table before us while we discuss, so far as we are able, the reasons and emotions which make us hesitate to sign it"

(123). Through truth-telling, the table becomes a site of further truth-telling that enables freedom: the outsider refusal to become part of any association.

However, turning the kitchen or dining-room or office or committee-room table into a site of truth-telling may also be risky, turning an ordinarily comfortable setting into a site of conflict, tension, and fear. For example, Woolf says:

> Let us suppose, then, that in the course of that bi-sexual private conversation about politics and people, war and peace, barbarism and civilization, some question has cropped up, about admitting, shall we say, the daughters of educated men to the Church or the Stock Exchange or the diplomatic service. The question is adumbrated merely; but we *on our side of the table* become aware at once of some "strong emotion" on your side "arising from some motive below the level of conscious thought" by the ringing of an alarm bell within us; a confused but tumultuous clamour: You shall not, you shall not, shall not . . . . (*TG*, 153)

Laying the photographs on the table may not always successfully disengage it from patriarchy and war. Even if the table becomes open to new possibilities through laying one's cards on it (so to speak), it may be re-mobilized as a site of conflict, war, and potential domination. Putting the photos on the table may thus exceed, while also in some sense remaining within, the patriarchal economy of war and force. Yet Woolf also seems to suggest that truth-telling—like the activities of the war society—may leave its own material residue and momentum: creating places (rooms, tables, neighborhoods) that are more amenable to freedom and truth-telling, that perhaps have more "corners" that outsiders might occupy, or that are haunted by the "ghosts" of truth-tellers like Chelsea Manning.

I am interested in the possibilities opened by Woolf's attention to the possible indeterminacy of the table: namely, that many spaces or locales may be open to such transformation and that truth-telling can transform a table from being a site of public or private discourse into a place of truth-telling which, while situated in war society, also provides an outsider place for telling the truth, a place where outsider truths *may* become significant.

LEAKY WARS, LEAKY DEVICES

If in the 1930s, everyone had their own table where they put their papers, in the early twenty-first century, many of us have devices—our phones, tablets, computers, Wifi-enabled televisions. Like tables, these devices can serve multiple purposes, moving from being sites of work to sites of commerce, to sites of intimacy, social coordination, or pleasure. While Woolf suggests that putting the war photos on the table can lift that table out of context, rendering it a site available for outsider truth-telling, I want to suggest here that Manning's release of the *Collateral Murder* footage lifts our devices, even if briefly, out of their assignment to their various functions (private, public, social, intimate, work, pleasure) and renders them visible as sites of *leaking*, sites where (as Wendy Chun argues) the cracks and connections between these realms appear and spaces for outsider truth-telling—which is not fully ascribable to any of these functions—may appear.

Incident in New Baghdad

On July 12, 2007, two Apache helicopters, associated with US Army company 2-16, shot and killed twelve men in New Baghdad, Iraq. Two of the men they killed were Reuters employees—a photographer (Namir Noor-Eldeen) and driver (Saeed Chmagh). They also wounded, and almost killed, two children who were in a van whose driver stopped to try to help Chmagh. The Apache gunner shot and killed the children's father, as well as the other individuals in the van and Chmagh. Soldiers on the Apache helicopters recorded all the video and audio footage from the attack, as David Finkel reports in his book on 2-16, *The Good Soldiers*.[19] After realizing that they had killed two Reuters employees, the commander of Company 2-16, Ralph Kauzlarich, judged that they had obeyed the rules of engagement and put the matter aside. While Reuters repeatedly asked for an investigation, and tried to obtain the video footage via a Freedom of Information Act request, the US Army maintained that there was no wrongdoing and refused to release the footage.

On February 10, 2010, Chelsea Manning leaked the footage of the July 2007 Apache incident to Wikileaks. About three months later, on April 5, 2010, Julian Assange held a press conference and released the decoded version to the public on the Wikileaks website. The raw footage that Manning sent to Wikileaks was thirty-nine minutes long. Along with it, Wikileaks released a shorter, edited version of the video, which they entitled *Collateral Murder*. In both versions, the viewer sees and hears the soldiers in the Apache kill the two sets of Iraqis: first, a group of men they believe to be armed with AK-47s and RPGs; and second, a group of people in a van who try to help a wounded man. In the unedited version, the viewer also sees the Apache go on to fire several Hellfire missiles into a building, in which the pilots claim there are several armed men; this incident does not appear in the edited version.[20] In the edited version, the viewer is given more context for the footage, and the events are framed through the lens of a clear political agenda (the video begins with a quote from George Orwell: "Political language is designed to make lies sound truthful and murder respectable, and to give the appearance of solidity to pure wind"). The edited version also superimposes arrows on the video that show who the Reuters employees are and point out the children in the van. In both versions of the video, we see US soldiers running with the two wounded children to their tanks and asking that the children be evacuated to their base, Rustamaya. This request was denied, and the children were taken to a local Iraqi hospital.

Most news articles about the release of the *Collateral Murder* footage focus on the actions that the army could take, plans to take, or might have taken in response to the events depicted therein; news coverage also examined the new way in which the footage was released, that is, directly to the public via the Wikileaks site instead of being filtered through journalistic judgment. Thus, in Elizabeth Bumiller's article in the *New York Times*, she notes that, "The American military in Baghdad investigated the episode and concluded that the forces involved had no reason to know that there were Reuters employees in the group. No disciplinary action was taken." She goes on to offer quotes from military officials about why they believed the soldiers' actions were justified: United States Central Command "stated that the Reuters employees 'made no effort to visibly display their status as press or media representatives and their familiar behavior with, and close proximity to, the armed insurgents and their furtive attempts to photograph the coalition ground forces made them appear as hostile combatants to the Apaches that engaged them.'"[21] Other articles on the incident ask whether the soldiers followed the Rules of Engagement, which include rules of proportionality, positive identification, and respect for those ("friend or foe") trying to assist the wounded.[22] In other words, the press response to the release of the video largely fit it into a conventional whistleblower frame, where the release of information is supposed to be used to check abuses, demand accountability, and return organizations to a respect for rules and laws.

This, of course, did not happen. The release of the *Collateral Murder* footage did not produce any visible reforms, and no one was held accountable. By the whistleblower standard, in other words, the release of the footage was a failure. In what follows, I suggest that while the Wikileaks editing of the footage in the shorter version prompts its audience to see its import in traditional whistleblower terms—and thus sets us up for failure—the raw footage reveals more transformational possibilities implicit in the leaking, and helps me to develop an alternative framework for judging its success or failure. In particular, I suggest that it reveals the leakiness of the war, itself—the leakiness between the perspective of the soldier and the perspective of the civilian and between public and private (evident in the language used by the soldiers, as well as by the collapse between combatant/non-combatant, battlefield/home, that is obvious in the video). If Woolf portrays the outsider on a "bridge," the raw *Collateral Murder* footage positions us in the space of the leak, unable to be contained within a particular sphere or realm, within either war or peace, yet connected to both.

As sites of leakiness, our devices become neither sites of private intimacy and sociality, which must be secured from the governmental gaze, nor sites of political action and publicity; they become, rather—even if only briefly—sites that betray the limits of the norms and rules of both public and private spheres to address the oppressions and suffering we see in the video footage. As sites of leaking, our devices call us to see the *Collateral Murder* video footage—as Woolf says we see the Spanish Civil War photos—as having a figure superimposed over it, the figure (here) of us, of both complicity in the wrong and the possibility to change things.

The Video(s)

In the edited version of *Collateral Murder*, the viewer is offered an interpretive frame through which to view the shooting of twelve people. At the beginning of the video, after the quote from Orwell, a description of the events in the footage appears on the screen: "On the morning of July 12th, 2007, two Apache helicopters using 30mm cannon fire killed about a dozen people in the Iraqi suburb of New Baghdad. Two children were also wounded. Although some of the men appear to have been armed, the behavior of nearly everyone was relaxed. The US military initially claimed that all the dead were anti-Iraqi forces or 'insurgents.'" We are then informed that two of the dead were Reuters employees, shown photos of them, and also shown photos of one of the employee's grieving sons. Quickly on the heels of these photos and information, the screen fades to a quote from Lieutenant-Colonel Scott Belichwehl, spokesman for the US forces in Baghdad: "There is no question that coalition forces were clearly engaged in combat operations against a hostile force." The edited video then fades to a new script, informing us that the US military refused to release this footage, and it has been inaccessible to the public, "[u]ntil now." The implication is clear: the US military has covered up wrongdoing and lied about it. This video offers redress; it reveals and, in revealing, portrays itself as already a kind of action, which demands accountability. In Chun's terms, the *Collateral Murder* video asks its viewers to see the mere watching of the video as a way of being empowered, of acting to remedy the wrong that is revealed.

The edited version of the video has the advantage of including context, which allows casual viewers to understand what they are watching. Yet the edited version provides context only via a narrative that attempts to control the meaning of the depicted events. Specifically, in framing the import of the footage in traditional whistleblower terms, the edited version also encourages the viewer to understand themselves as un-implicated in the wrongs they view, as part of the group demanding redress and accountability from an army and government whose deception and abuses has resulted in all this death. The edited footage, in other words, encourages viewers to place responsibility on the army and to feel that, simply in watching the footage, they are participating in achieving justice for the dead and wounded.

The raw footage offers a different viewing experience, one that positions the viewer not as a citizen seeking accountability as part of a viewing public but rather in the space of the leak. The raw footage does this in three primary ways.

First, the raw footage reveals connections, and leakages, between the violences of (public) US militarism and of (private) American masculinity. Toward the end of the raw footage, for example, the Apache helicopter asks permission to fire a hellfire missile into a building that is either abandoned or under construction. The gunner has seen a few armed men walk into the building. We, the viewers, have also seen unarmed men walk into the building. The Apache receives permission to fire the missile. When they fire it, the gunner says, "There it goes. Look at that bitch go! Patoosh!" The gunner's words, omitted from the edited version, reveal (crudely and obviously) militaristic masculinity. What I want to emphasize here, however, is how both the firing of the missile—despite seeing unarmed men going into the building—and the derogatory feminization of the weapon fired, reflect an attempt to circumscribe or eradicate vulnerability. The soldier's comportment, structured around the violent eradication of possible threats (sacrificing the unarmed men in the building, in order to ensure a condition of supposed security for everyone), is connected to a certain form of masculinity: a form that understands femininity as a dangerous threat to masculine invulnerability and which may require violent domestication.

According to Gregoire Chamayou, the desire to become invulnerable is the mode of comportment of contemporary militarism more generally—of which the drone represents the paradigm. In contrast to the heroic ethos of classical and even in modern accounts of war, drone warfare emphasizes reducing risk and rendering soldiers invulnerable: "[s]elf-preservation by means of drones involves putting vulnerable bodies out of reach."[23] In this sense, drone warfare sits comfortably within neoliberalism and its reduction of political conflicts to issues of risk management, especially the management of risks to life.[24]

This form of militarist masculinity seems to govern the very way the gunner sees the world. In a telling moment (not included in the edited version) in between the shooting of the twelve men and the firing of the hellfire missiles, the gunner's gaze briefly swings around and settles on a veiled woman walking a child down the street; just as abruptly the camera swings away, without comment. He seems to be unable to apprehend individuals, the non-western woman and child, who are neither friend nor foe, neither ally nor threat. Rather, his vision is governed by his attempt to assure invulnerability. To return to the building into which he fires missiles, the Apache gunner's felt vulnerability to the men with weapons appears to make him literally incapable of seeing the unarmed men who walk into the building, as well as the unarmed civilians who are simply walking past the building into which he plans to fire missiles. In the last shot we see of the building before the missile explodes into it, we see a man simply walking past—a man who is apparently obliterated by the missile. The gunner does not seem to see or comprehend his existence; we do not see him again. The raw footage thus calls the viewer to see the entanglement of militarist and masculine desires for invulnerability and the costs of these desires—in actual violence, and in a violent comportment—for both public and private spheres.

Second, in contrast to the edited version which distances the viewer from the events contained in the footage through framing it with external narration, the raw footage puts the viewer directly into the pilot's perspective—not just because we are looking at the footage he recorded but because we are looking at it the same way he was: on a screen. We are viewing this footage on a computer, a phone, a television, a tablet; we are viewing it as a movie, just like the gunner. If Woolf putting war photos on the table pulled the table out of its established use and repurposed it as a site of truth-telling—revealing both our complicity and the possibility of change—Manning's release of the *Collateral Murder* footage (via Assange) pulls our devices out of their established uses, revealing them as sites of complicity and truth-telling. Looking at Iraq from an overhead perspective, through the cinematic lens of the gunner—recording/observation/violence entwined—we become a part of his desire for invulnerability. The consequences of this view are obvious in the video: death, wounded children, ruined houses, a comportment of anxiety and violence. Yet by revealing how our perspective—the very medium through which we receive news, engage in social media, send texts, receive calls— is entwined with, and complicit in, war and its violence, Manning's leaking begins to change the world by showing that this medium is violent *and* enabling of truth-telling, a way of hearing truth *and* a way of participating in violence.

Finally, the raw footage has no clear beginning and end, illustrating that there is no "incident in New Baghdad"; that "incident" is one blip in a chain of violences that never ends, generated by a need to assure invulnerability that will never end. In the raw footage, as in the edited version, the viewer sees the initial shooting of the group of men (including the Reuters employees) and then the shooting of the individuals in the van trying to assist a wounded man. Yet, in contrast to the edited version, after we see the drama of two soldiers running with wounded children from the van to the tanks, and after we watch the tanks depart, we see life start to resume on the streets. Cars and people go by. Then the soldiers fire three hellfire missiles into the building. The raw footage ends after the third hellfire missile is fired, without offering us a clear ending or conclusion to what we have seen. In contrast to the edited version, then, there is no clean bounding of a singular event—to which it is then possible to render justice. Instead, the raw footage leaks at the seams, suggesting that if we kept watching, we would see more of the same—the killing of people who may or may not be hostile to soldiers, the destruction of homes and families. This is not a discrete event. Rather, this leaking, this lack of a conclusion to the killing, is the war.

In contrast to the edited version, then, the raw footage positions viewers less as innocent citizens demanding accountability from guilty elites (who would not provide it) and more as a *part of*, or complicit in, the violence they are witnessing. Revealing our perspective (on our devices) to leak into the gunner's, the raw footage lifts our devices out of their normal functions and renders them available for new kinds of uses, communication, and connections. In so doing, the raw footage calls us to see the connections between violence abroad and at home, between the masculine desire for invulnerability in war and in the domestic sphere, and between our digital gaze (that seeks to contain, and render safe, what we see on our devices) and the gaze of the gunner, which seeks to avoid or obliterate that which disrupts its violent strategies of containment. On this reading, our devices change, becoming sites—like Woolf's table—of both implication in violence and the freedom to act differently.

"[W]HAT ARE WE DOING THERE?"

On April 5, 2010, Ethan McCord, a veteran of the Iraq war who had been part of Company 2-16, came home after dropping off his children at school. Turning on the news (as he always did), McCord later recounted that he was shocked to see an image of himself running and carrying a wounded child from a van in New Baghdad to his tank. In an interview in the documentary, *Incident in New Baghdad*, McCord said, "I knew it was me because that image is burned into my head. The smells came back to me, the cries of the child came back to me." McCord said of this first viewing of the footage, "I was really angry because I had tried to put that behind me and not think about it." His television and living room were transformed by the footage from being a space of apparent safety (of retreat from the war) into a space of risk and leakage between war and peace, public and private—where he was recalled to his participation in the Iraq war.

While this leakage felt dangerous, it also enabled and called him to address those events and his participation in them, in ways he had previously felt powerless to pursue. McCord suddenly became leaky himself; he began talking. He gave interviews about the events of that day, and about his views of the war. He re-connected with another veteran from his unit, Josh Steiger, and with him wrote an "Open Letter of Reconciliation and Responsibility to the Iraqi People."[25] He gave an interview to a filmmaker that became the Academy Award nominated short documentary *Incident in New Baghdad*.

In these various interviews and writings, McCord described in detail his experience of that day as a turning point in his time in the army. Having joined the army hoping to do good, McCord reports that, "I had it in my head that we're in Iraq for a good cause; we're here to help the Iraqi people . . . Our mission is to provide stability for the Iraqi people, and that's what I wanted to do . . . I wanted to be the guy the Iraqis were cheering for as I drove down the road."[26] This attitude started to shift when one of his good friends,

Andre Craig, was killed by a bomb, an improvised explosive device (IED). Then came July 10, 2007. McCord was part of the ground unit called in after the Apache shot the twelve men and wounded the two children.

When he arrived, he saw a group of men lying by the wall along with an anti-tank weapon, an RPG. He said that at the time, "they didn't look human to me; they looked like something out of a horror movie . . . It just didn't seem real." Then, McCord said, he "could hear a child crying." It was coming from the van. Another soldier got to the van first, looked inside, and started to throw up. McCord said, "[w]hat he saw inside were the children." The "little girl, about 3 or 4 years old, . . . had a wound to her belly. She had glass in her eyes and in her hair. She had a bunch of little scratches and cuts. Right next to her, and half on the floorboards, with his head on the seat, was a little boy, about seven or eight. I thought he was dead; he wasn't moving or breathing. Next to him, was who I assumed was the father"—who was dead. McCord says that "[w]hen I first pulled the girl out, and I had her in my arms, cradling her, it's kind of weird to explain it, but I almost felt as if I was holding my own child . . . The emotions that were rushing through me, it was very emotional for me, because my son was born, just prior to this, and my daughter was close to the same age, and I kept picturing my own children." After the medic takes the girl to evacuate her, McCord says that he saw the boy take a breath, and he started screaming, "The boy's alive, the boy's alive." "I grabbed him, picked him up, told him everything's gonna be okay, and started running towards the Bradley [tank]."[27]

McCord says that he hadn't really processed how or why the children had been shot, but he assumed that it must have been the guys with the RPG. "I put myself in denial that . . . American troops could do this to innocent children." Later, he pieced things together and realized it was the Apaches. "Things from that day," McCord said, "changed for me. I no longer felt that I was doing good in Iraq." He tried to see a mental health professional, but his commanding officer told him to "suck it up; quit being a pussy; get the sand out of your vagina."[28] In other words, render yourself invulnerable. McCord did not go for psychiatric help. When he returned to Wichita, he suffered from post-traumatic stress disorder (PTSD), drank heavily, and felt that he was destroying his family. Eventually McCord began therapy and started to feel like he was processing his anger and guilt, but seeing the video footage interrupted his attempt to put the war behind him and called him to participate in a new scene in which he might tell the truth.

Indeed, the core of what McCord had to say after watching the *Collateral Murder* footage was less about the specific incident documented and more about the devastation of waging war in Iraq in general and our complicity in it. McCord said, "I didn't pull the trigger that day. I didn't shoot those children. I didn't shoot their father. But I am a part of that system that killed those people . . . I think every American is a part of that system . . . But if everybody was to stand up and say, this is bullshit, no more, we're not gonna do it anymore . . . , then it'd make a big difference."[29] For McCord, in other words, the point is not to call the army to account for their abuses but to change the world: to end the wars and war culture that killed so many people on behalf of a mythical invulnerability—a mythic character testified to by McCord's own broken self.

McCord's response to *Collateral Murder*, and the further public speech and connections that speech generated between him and other anti-war soldiers, suggests that Manning's leaking of the footage was significant in ways that the whistleblower/accountability script misses, but which the perspective gleaned from Woolf and the raw footage helps us to elucidate. In particular, that perspective suggests that Manning's leaking should be judged not only in terms of formal accountability within a military that Woolf indicts as oppressive as such, but also in terms of whether that leaking begins to change the world, so as to enable further truth-telling (rather than war). Indeed, McCord's interviews and speeches about the war called less for accountability from elites for the particular events of July 10, 2007—and some of the specifics of McCord's own account of that date have been contested[30]—and more for broad public accountability for what war does to Iraqis and soldiers, and for the war to stop. McCord's actions reveal that Manning's leaking *did* transform the world, at least a bit, to enable some (like McCord) to begin to offer their own truths to that new world under construction, to offer their reality as a way of constructing a world without war. McCord's speech, sparked by Manning's leaking, begins to change the world some more. Indeed, as McCord says in a *Wired* interview, "I've spoken with other soldiers who were there. Some of them [say] I don't care what anybody says . . . they're not there. . . . There's also some soldiers who joke about it [as a] coping mechanism. They're like, oh yeah, we're the "collateral murder" company. I don't think that [the] big picture is whether or not [the Iraqis who were killed] had weapons. I think that the bigger picture is what are we doing there? We've been there for so long now and it seems like nothing is being accomplished whatsoever, except for we're making more people hate us."[31] McCord's hard, contested conversations with other soldiers and

veterans—like Woolf's with men around the dinner table—
do not eradicate a world of war but rather display (in part
via his recounting of it in *Wired* online and elsewhere) that
the world *is already changing*, that people like McCord and
Manning (and Woolf) are already at work on constructing
a new world that is productively unsettling patriarchy and
militarism.

CONCLUSION

Chelsea Manning's leaking of *Collateral Murder* did not bring
justice to the families of those killed and wounded on July 7,
2010; nor did it call any individuals within the army to account
for their deaths. But it did change the world, transforming—
and continuing to transform—devices and the spaces in
which they are located (living rooms, classrooms, offices,
the street down which we're walking) into sites of leakage
and vulnerability, complicity and truth-telling. This kind of
transformation invites, and even demands, a certain kind of
truth-telling—not the expert recitation of statistics or the as-
sessment of risk or justification in the soldiers' actions, but
the leaky truth-telling of outsiders: a form of speech that has
no sanction from public or private authorities, which reveals
the oppressions of both while calling us to acknowledge that
we are all within the system and, to differing degrees, respon-
sible for it.

Manning's leaking, among other effects, transformed
McCord's living room and, in turn, his life; McCord's truth-
telling, disseminated through interviews, open letters, and
documentaries, intervened in public life and called some of
his fellow veterans to tell their truth, their reality. This chain

of truth-telling and world-changing offers an example of the material, worldly residue of truth-telling that I found in Woolf's stacking of war photos on the table. While we tend to look for the impact of truth-telling in our institutions, officials, and laws, I have suggested that it may be equally important to think about how truth-telling may be at work in changing the world in more horizontal, material ways— transforming our devices, houses, workplaces, and streets in ways that enable other outsiders to speak of their realities.

This conception of truth-telling presents it neither as an individual ethics nor as a collective politics, but as a *scene* that outsider truth-tellers (try to) create—a scene that, in turn, might summon new actors, actions, and plots into being, some of which may be political, some of which may be art or literature, and some of which may involve the individual's soul or internal life. In this sense, Woolf, Manning, and McCord all challenge us to imagine how we might create places and spaces where, through sharing truths with others, we might begin to imagine and act differently: finding the courage to acknowledge complicity in, and also demand something beyond, the institutions and habits of patriarchal militarism.

"I USED TO ONLY KNOW

HOW TO WRITE MEMOS"

The World-Building Power of Outsider Security

OUTSIDER TRUTH-TELLERS REVEAL THAT THE dominant system of representing truth sanctions and serves the hierarchies and violence of the war society. The narrow, abstract "facts" demanded by security-oriented and risk-averse institutions demand in turn a certain kind of speaker: the dispassionate, masculine figure, who sacrifices his private desires on behalf of the public good. The demand for facts, and the speakers who speak them, generates information and subject positions (e.g., scientists telling the truth about climate change) crucial to democracy. Yet this system of representing truth is also, and at the same time, antidemocratic: not only in the exclusivity of its model of truth (precise, narrow) and truth-teller (gendered, raced, classed) but *also* in its narrow portrayal of security as generated by acquiescence to elite determinations about whose reality, and which facts, matter for politics.

Outsider truth-tellers offer, in contrast, *insurgent truth*: the narrative, unwieldy, excessive truths of complex worldliness. Their lived truthfulness is not so easily read: it generates new figures of legibility and credibility and contributes to a world that is not yet fully built. Rather than seeking to tailor their reality to a system of representation in which they will never be hearable anyway, outsider truth-tellers situate reality in new stagings: how masculine militarism looks from a female literary perspective (Woolf); how the war in Iraq appears to a queer gender-non-conforming soldier (Manning); or how a gunner's perspective looks on an iPhone (*Collateral Murder*). Refusing recognition on a common ground that often works to exclude them, outsider truth-tellers call us to position ourselves in the not yet fully legible stagings, scenes, and lived enactments of reality that outsiders offer us. Outsider truth-tellers, of whom there is surely a larger cohort than the few examined here, ask us to find ways to speak to each other within the context of different scenes, even if we do not fully understand them, and to acknowledge how the dominant system of representing truth in fact leaves many outside its circle of hear-ability.

Pundits and theorists who have dubbed our era a "post-truth age" may see my argument for outsider truth-telling as contributing to, rather than describing, the disintegration of the common ground offered by basic facts.[1] Indeed, some have suggested that a "postmodern" approach to truth, which claims objectivity and facts are historically constructed, itself underwrites the post-truth era.[2] By showing that the modern fact is only one, historically situated way to represent reality, historians like Poovey, Lorraine Daston, and Shapin (and theorists like me) have on this account injected facts with doubt and skepticism and thus created an environment where someone like Trump could thrive. These kinds of claims accord a great deal of power to academic writing—could such critics cause the loss of faith in facts, really?—and go farther than Poovey and the others in suggesting that truth is not just represented in historically contingent ways but *can* be dissolved. This critique is, in other words, nihilistic in ways that Poovey and other historians' claims about historically constituted *modes* of representing truth is not.

I hope to have offered here a more hopeful possibility than this view or the more general view that we have entered a "post-truth" age. Showing the exclusivity and violences of our truth-security regime, I am suggesting that if that regime is currently under pressure, it may be due not *only* to would-be authoritarians like Trump who are not concerned with truth but perhaps *also* to more politically promising pressure that outsider truth-telling exerts on an exclusive, hierarchical truth-security regime. If agreement over facts appears to be in decline, we had better ask whether that means that truth itself is in decline or whether a modern system of representing truth—which relied on capitalism, racial hierarchies, and patriarchy—is in crisis. If we see it as the latter, we may be better able to decenter Trump (and the academics) from our picture of the contemporary relationship between truth and politics and examine Trump's disregard for facts as one node in a broader crisis, in which the modern system for representing truth is also coming under pressure in ways that might prove more promising.

Indeed, we can see this more promising pressure, for example, in the rising public attention given to, and protest surrounding, the reluctance of institutions, prosecutors, police, judges, and juries to believe women who claim they have been raped or sexually assaulted.[3] We can see it in the widespread public protests—epitomized by the Black Lives Matter movement—over the failure of juries, members of the public, and prosecutors to believe that photographic/video evidence of police killing people of color shows racially biased murder.[4] We can see it in the public debates over President Obama's commutation of Chelsea Manning's sentence. While every day many white, cis-gender men are taken as real truth-tellers and members of marginalized groups are portrayed as unreliable speakers, this system of representing truth also appears to be under immense pressure.

This means that our current moment is one of danger *and* promise. Some (such as Trump) certainly disregard facts as a way of attempting to *create* a reality that never was, where white people were fully dominant, women happily served as subordinates to men, and immigrants were kept in orderly submission. Yet others productively challenge an order of representing truth that privileges the speech of white cis-gender men over women, people of color, and sexually and gender-non-conforming individuals. One implication of all of this is that criticizing Trump primarily in terms of his avoidance of facts, correcting him on the facts, may be less productive than focusing on the *substantive* problem with his approach: that it is racist, sexist, quasi-fascist, and violently xenophobic. Many prefer the critique of him as untruthful because it appears—like facts—to offer a common ground in a democracy of diverse interests. Yet as I have suggested, this notion of facts offering a pre-political common ground is premised on a hierarchal system of representing truth indexed to class, race, gender, and sexuality. Democracy needs more than facts and a willingness to debate on this (un)common ground. Indicting Trump in terms of the world he seeks to create (white, sexist, unequal, xenophobic) gestures toward the richer vision democracy needs, connecting the facts to outsider truth-telling and democratic demands for what could be: a world of equality, freedom, the generous treatment of immigrants, egalitarian pleasure, and a reality inflected and enriched by diverse experiences and narratives.

Outsider truth-telling provides a critique of dominant conventions of truth-telling, but it also offers alternative precedents for representing truth—precedents that are sorely needed in our current moment. Far from discarding the security that truth is supposed to provide, I want to suggest in this final section that outsider truth-telling generates a different kind of security: one that acknowledges its own partiality and riskiness and is achieved through connections with others who lend significance to one's actions, speech, suffering, and struggles. This is a security provided not by agreement (compelled by self-evidence) or violence but instead by the pleasures of sharing and taking up a role in someone else's depiction of reality. I describe this kind of outsider security via a brief discussion of Chelsea Manning's prison writings, focusing especially on those pieces in which her connections with other prisoners are highlighted.

OUTSIDER SECURITY

While in prison, Manning wrote columns for *The Guardian* newspaper. Those articles revolved primarily around four or five distinct topics: war/the military, the politics of whistleblowing, prison experiences, and trans and queer politics. But there is a basic claim that holds these different pieces together: security is achieved not through a national security state primed for (and engaged in) war on and surveillance of outsiders but rather through collective connections that resist state attempts to separate and surveil us.[5] Echoing the pacifist point that increased militarization renders us less, not more, secure, Manning criticizes responses to the 2016 mass shooting in the gay Florida nightclub, Pulse, (in a June 13, 2016 piece) that seek to heighten surveillance on marginalized communities, or pursue "anti-Muslim foreign policy." For Manning, turning to law enforcement or the military to achieve security only makes marginalized groups less secure and proliferates marginalization through ever-more expansive practices of profiling. She says, "Any increase in surveillance of marginalized communities for the sake of security thereafter have expanded the cycle of criminalization that queer people—especially queer people of color—are forced to navigate."[6]

Manning brings these arguments together in an essay she wrote for *Captive Genders*, an important edited volume focused on the relationship between trans* people and the prison. There, Manning builds on the work of CeCe McDonald and other trans* prison activists (also in the volume) and draws attention to the connections between the military-industrial and prison-industrial complexes, arguing that they both work to surveil, discipline, and segregate certain populations—especially the most marginalized—from others.[7] For example, Manning argues that both systems negatively impact youth offenders, especially low-income youth and youth of color. "Many youth, even those who are first time offenders, become caught in a cycle of release and re-offense. Vulnerable youth also get caught up in the military-industrial complex: there is the enlistment of sailors, soldiers, airmen, and marines, and their placement into harm's way."[8]

Women and "other gender and sexual minorities" are also negatively affected by the disciplinary "imposition of strict gender norms of femininity on women, and the praise of masculinity and the macho at the expense of femininity, which is deemed a sign of 'weakness.'"[9] These systems put money into "police stations, jails, prisons, and parole offices at home, and ships and military bases overseas," rather than into the social programs that would help people live meaningful lives. Thus, the military and the prison conspire to create a condition of "security" that actually generates deep insecurity—psychologically, socially, and bodily—for certain marginalized populations, including those not actually institutionalized. Members of marginalized groups, such as Manning, are put into "the exhausting and dehumanizing position of being determined as a potential criminal, threat to national security, and—ironically—be deemed immutably male."[10] Once these practices raise the fear factor, mainstreamed populations are also governed by fear and sensitized to insecurity.

Instead of turning to the state (and its prisons and military) to offer security,[11] Manning argues that true security comes into being through creating connections with others that allow us to live and identify ourselves truthfully. As she puts it in her piece on the Pulse shootings, "[w]e are not safe and secure when the government uses us as pawns to perpetrate violence against others. Our safety and security will come when we organize, love and resist together."[12] This "joy, confidence and security can't begin until we are able to just be ourselves" because insofar as we are separated and categorized based on oppressive social categories, there will always be the risk of violence and of addressing that risk by turning to more violence in the form of the security state.[13]

Manning offers a few suggestions about how we might pursue this alternative form of security. In her *Captive Genders* essay, Manning says that we can respond to the condition of insecurity created by the state's social categorizations through "communicat[ing] with each other, sharing knowledge, experience, ideas, and criticisms with each other. Through this kind of communication, which institutions naturally and reflexively attempt to stifle, we can help to regulate the expansion of and to minimize the scale and effect of the military and prison industrial complexes in our lives."[14]

Manning offers models of this kind of outsider education, communication, and support from her experiences in the site she also identifies as disciplinary, exclusionary, and oppressive: the prison. For example, in "Prison Keeps Us Isolated. But Sometimes Sisterhood Can Bring Us Together,"[15] Manning describes an important friendship with another trans woman, whom she calls Alice. Despite attempts to keep them separate, Manning and Alice were able to find ways to connect at Fort Leavenworth, and their friendship was a source of empowerment in each one's quest to receive proper medical care while in prison. When they first encountered each other in the prison dining hall, Alice "hurriedly and excitedly approached" Manning "and described at machine-gun speed her own battle to receive healthcare, and how her enthusiasm to continue was re-ignited by my own efforts." Manning offered to help Alice by showing her how to pursue the bureaucratic requests for care and "how to petition for a change of name." Prison administrators responded to this friendship by attempting to transfer both prisoners elsewhere (but they only succeeded in transferring Alice). A few weeks after the American Civil Liberties Union (ACLU) submitted a demand on Manning's behalf, Manning says, "my best friend and ally at the prison was suddenly approached by prison officials on her way to work one morning. They pulled Alice aside and told her that she was going back to her cell to gather her belongings and 'pack out.'" Manning learned of Alice's departure only by seeing her "pushing a large cart filled with what few belongings she had, looking scared but confident." But Manning and Alice were able to enact a quick gesture of solidarity: "a quick high five, a sad head-nod and a little wave." In this story, the prison isolates and oppresses the marginalized, but it also occasions connection. While prison administrators here get their way, Manning's narration of her friendship with Alice sounds a note of hope: the high five, head-nod, and wave disclose an outsider repertoire of world-building that they carry with them even as they are separated.

In her last column before her release, Manning wrote a letter of thanks to her fellow prisoners:

> When the prison tried to break one of us, we all stood up. We looked out for each other. When they tried to divide us, and systematically discriminated against us, we embraced our diversity and pushed back. But, I also learned from all of you when to pick my battles. I grew up and grew connected because of the community you provided. Those outside of prison may not believe that we act like human beings under these conditions. But of course we do. And we build our own networks of survival . . . The most important thing that you taught me was how to write and how to speak in my own voice. I used to only know how to write memos. Now, I write like a human being, with dreams, desires and connections. I could not have done it without you.[16]

Manning's fellow prisoners taught her how to write "like a human being." In Quashie's terms, they helped her to be quiet—to find, explore, and express her humanity in terms that exceed or stand to the side of norms of public expressiveness. Here, the refusal to be identified as a certain kind of public self is part of a practice of creating new worlds and connections. While those worlds have a public dimension, as with Manning's very public demands for appropriate treatment as a trans woman in prison, they also consist in ties of quiet, of pleasure and joy, and of styles of being that exceed dominant norms of recognition and resistance. Like Rustin, Manning's persistence is quiet not in the sense of silent, but in the sense of refusing a certain kind of audibility and hear-ability: her writings display her idiosyncratic humanity, desires, joys, pleasures, pains, and her practice of creative solidarity.

Manning's description of outsider world-building in prison calls to mind Christa Wolf's depiction of Cassandra's truth-telling as enabled by a secret women's collective centered in a cave outside the boundaries of Troy, which I discussed in the preface. For both Manning and Wolf's Cassandra, truth-telling is rendered possible not through solitary thought and retreat, but through the connection through and across difference that Audre Lorde says enables the "I to be." In the modern carceral state, however, outsider truth-telling as and through world-building appears less as a practice of speaking truth to power *from* the outside, where truth remains pure, fundamentally in opposition to hierarchy, and hence completely illegible to it (to the men of Troy and the Hellenes, Cassandra appeared to speak only gibberish). Instead, outsider truth-telling in Manning's prison, as on Woolf's bridge and in Cooper's corner, appears as a practice that emerges *within* power, vulnerable to its risks, hierarchies, and allure, and that promises not to transcend but create possibilities of transforming it. Outsider truth-tellers are not saints; they make mistakes, political and personal,[17] and they are shaped by power and invested in it even as they try to refuse absorption in its terms. Yet it is because their acts of truth-telling are very human, messy, complex, and situated that their practice reveals an alternative model of what truth-telling could be for our own time: a practice of creating connections through refusing absorption in public and private realms that also shape outsiders' speech and existence, and collectively creating new scenes of reality that make different forms of politics, and publics, possible.

NOTES

Preface: Cassandra and Socrates

1. For example, in "Letter from a Birmingham Jail," Martin Luther King Jr. writes: "Just as Socrates felt that it was necessary to create a tension in the mind so that individuals could rise from the bondage of myths and half truths to the unfettered realm of creative analysis and objective appraisal, so must we see the need for nonviolent gadflies to create the kind of tension in society that will help men rise from the dark depths of prejudice and racism to the majestic heights of understanding and brotherhood" (*A Testament to Hope*, ed. James Melon Washington. San Francisco: Harper and Row, 1986, 291). On Socrates, Thoreau, and especially Gandhi, see Alex Livingston's "Fidelity to Truth: Gandhi and the Genealogy of Civil Disobedience" (in *Political Theory* 2018 46(4): 511–536).

2. Arendt writes, for example, "Socrates wanted to make the city more truthful by delivering each of the citizens of their truths" (in "Philosophy and Politics," in *Social Research* 57(1990):1, 73–103, 81). For Michel Foucault on Socrates, see, for example, *The Government of Self and Others*, trans. Graham Burchell. (New York: Picador, 2011). On Socrates as an exemplar of democratic citizenship, see, for example, Joel Schlosser's *What Would*

Socrates Do? (Cambridge: Cambridge University Press, 2017) and Dana Villa's *Socratic Citizenship* (Princeton: Princeton University Press, 2001).

3. Arendt views the Socratic pursuit of non-contradiction as an inherently political project of educating citizens into virtue: "Socrates relied on two insights, the one being contained in the word of the Delphic Apollo, *gnothi sauthon,* know thyself, and the other related by Plato (and echoed in Aristotle): 'It is better to be in disagreement with the whole world than, being one, to be in disagreement with myself.' The latter is the key sentence for the Socratic conviction that virtue can be taught and learned" ("Philosophy and Politics," 85).

4. Aeschylus. *The Oresteia,* trans. Robert Fagles. New York: Penguin, 1984, lines 1211–1218. In the *Agamemnon,* while Clytemnestra is inside, preparing Agamemnon's and Cassandra's murders, Cassandra tells the Chorus of old men precisely what would happen: "slaughterhouse of heroes, soil streaming blood" (ibid., 1091); and a bit further: *"she gores him through!/*And now he buckles, look, the bath swirls red—/There's stealth and murder in the cauldron, do you hear?" (1129–1131). Yet the Chorus is unable to understand. The Chorus and its Leader say things like: "I can't read these signs" (1106); "Still lost. Her riddles, her dark words of god—/I'm groping, helpless" (1113–1114); and at their most perceptive, they say, "I'm not judge, I've little skill with the oracles,/but even I know danger when I hear it" (1132–1133).

5. On the genealogy of civil disobedience, see Livingston, "Fidelity to Truth."

6. Unlike Cassandra, Socrates was always supported by an elite group of men, over and against the view of the majority.

7. Some legal scholars have long used Cassandra to exemplify this problem. See, for example, Amy D. Ronner's "The Cassandra Curse: The Stereotype of the Female Liar Resurfaces in *Jones v. Clinton*" (in U.C. Davis Law Review 31 (1997)). Similarly, see Marilyn Yarbrough and Crystal Bennett's "Cassandra and the 'Sistahs': The Peculiar Treatment of African American Women in the Myth of Women as Liars" (in *Journal of Gender, Race, and Justice* 3 (2000): 625–657).

8. I am not the first to draw attention to such hierarchies of truth. Elizabeth Markovits notes in *The Politics of Sincerity* (State College: Penn State Press, 2010), for example, that dominant norms of truth-telling "privilege a stereotypically masculine style of talk—self-confidence, certainty, and a seemingly dispassionate tone [that] demonstrate the speaker's commitment to the discussion" (34). Similarly, Utz McKnight argues in *Race and the Politics of Exception* (New York: Routledge, 2013) that blacks are not allowed to "defin[e] the truth of racism" (67), and that they must defer to dominant groups to validate their articulation of their own experience (70–72). See also Leigh Gilmore's *Tainted Witness: Why We Doubt What Women Say About Their Lives* (New York: Columbia University Press, 2017).
9. For example, in their edited volume, *Myth and Violence in the Contemporary Female Text: New Cassandras* (London: Ashgate, 2011), Sanja Bajun-Radunovic and V. G. Julie Rajan use the figure of Cassandra to illuminate and show connections between diverse attempts of female authors, and the texts they create, to reveal reality to the public about ecological threats, patriarchal violence, war, and queer struggle (6).
10. For an excellent, historically grounded, argument for the significance of the Black Lives Matter movement, see Keeanga Yahmatta-Taylor's *From Black Lives Matter to Black Liberation* (Chicago: Haymarket Books, 2017).
11. See, for example, Arendt, "Philosophy and Politics"; Foucault, *The Government of Self and Others*; Schlosser, *What Would Socrates Do?*; Villa, *Socratic Citizenship*; and J. Peter Euben's *Corrupting Youth: Political Education, Democratic Culture, and Political Theory* (Princeton: Princeton University Press, 1997).
12. Christa Wolf. *Cassandra*, trans. Jan Van Heurk. New York: Farrar, Straus, and Giroux, 1988.

Chapter 1

1. Of her decision to change her name legally to Chelsea, Pfc. Manning writes that it is "a far better, richer, and more honest

reflection of who I am and always have been: a woman named Chelsea." See her "A Statement on My Legal Name Change" (in *The Huffington Post*. Posted April 23, 2014. http://www. huffingtonpost.com/chelsea-manning/a-statement-on-my-legal-name-change_b_5199874.html. Accessed April 28, 2014).

2. The leaked documents are available at wardiaries.wikileaks. org, wikileaks.org/plusd/, and collateralmurder.wikileaks. org. Helpful pieces on the key takeaways from the Iraq War Logs can be found in "Wikileaks Iraq War Logs: Key Findings," *The Telegraph* (https://www.telegraph.co.uk/news/ worldnews/middleeast/iraq/8085076/Wikileaks-Iraq-war-logs-key-findings.html. Published October 25, 2010. Accessed September 16, 2018) and various visualizations of the data from the Iraq war logs, such as the *New York Times*' "A Deadly Day in Baghdad" (https://archive.nytimes.com/www.nytimes. com/interactive/2010/10/24/world/1024-surge-graphic.html. Published 2010. Accessed September 16, 2018.)

3. "Manning-Lamo Chat Logs Revealed," Wired. July 13, 2011 (http://www.wired.com/threatlevel/2011/07/manning-lamo-logs; Accessed January 30, 2013).

4. For example, see: Glenn Greenwald's "Manning Deserves a Medal" (in *The Guardian*. www.guardian.co.uk/commentisfree/ 2011/dec/14/bradley-manning-deserves-a-medal. Published December 14, 2011. Accessed March 15, 2013) and Chase Madar's "Manning, American Hero" (in *Le Monde Diplomatique*. https:// mondediplo.com/openpage/bradley-manning-american-hero. Published July 19, 2011. Accessed September 12, 2018). I discuss this in more depth in chapter 3.

5. Thanks to Brittney Cooper and her use of the word germinal in *Beyond Respectability: The Intellectual Thought of Race Women* (Champaign-Urbana: University of Illinois Press, 2017), for inspiring me to use "germinal" instead of "seminal."

6. Hannah Arendt. "Truth in Politics," in *Between Past and Future*. New York: Penguin, 1961, 1993, 264. Similarly, she says, "Even if we admit that every generation has the right to write its own history, we admit no more than that it has the right to rearrange the facts in accordance with its own perspective; we don't admit the right to touch the factual matter itself" (238–239).

NOTES | 151

For further explorations of this Arendtian approach to truth and politics, see *Truth and Democracy*, ed. Jeremy Elkins and Andrew Norris. Philadelphia: University of Pennsylvania Press, 2012.

7. Bernard Williams. *Truth and Truthfulness*. Princeton: Princeton University Press, 2004.

8. Michiko Kakutani. *The Death of Truth: Notes on Falsehood in the Age of Trump*. New York: Tim Duggan Books, 2018, 19, 23. See also Lee McIntyre. *Post-Truth*. Cambridge: MIT Press, 2018; and Kurt Andersen. *Fantasyland: How America Went Haywire*. New York: Random House, 2017.

9. Jason Stanley, "Beyond Lying: Trump's Authoritarian Reality," in *The New York Times*. https://www.nytimes.com/2016/11/05/opinion/beyond-lying-donald-trumps-authoritarian-reality.html. Published November 4, 2016. Accessed September 16, 2018. Similarly, writing in the *New York Times* before the election, William Davies argues that we are now living in an era of "data" rather than "facts": an era when our numbers give us "indicators of current sentiment" rather than help us "achieve consensus on the nature of social, economic, or environmental problems." William Davies, "The Age of Post-Truth Politics," in *The New York Times*, August 24, 2016. https://www.nytimes.com/2016/08/24/opinion/campaign-stops/the-age-of-post-truth-politics.html?_r=0. Accessed July 27, 2017. And in the *Daily Beast*, Touré writes that the goal of Trump and his coterie "is to delegitimize media. If there's no trust in media then there's no objective broker of facts and then you've successfully destabilized the truth. You've created a climate where there are no agreed upon facts and no objective truth." Touré. "The Liar-in-Chief and the Dangers of Post-Truth Politics," in *The Daily Beast*, March 18, 2017. http://www.thedailybeast.com/the-liar-in-chief-and-the-dangers-of-post-truth-politics. Accessed July 27, 2017. These are obviously just the tip of the iceberg of popular diagnoses of a "post-truth" age.

10. "Post-Truth Politics: The Art of the Lie," *The Economist*, September 10, 2016. https://www.economist.com/news/leaders/21706525-politicians-have-always-lied-does-it-matter-if-they-leave-truth-behind-entirely-art. Accessed July 27, 2017.

11. Steven Shapin. *A Social History of Truth: Civility and Science in Seventeenth Century England*. Chicago: University of Chicago Press, 1994, 202.
12. Ibid., 241–242. Gentlemen were regarded as credible because "[f]ree action and integrity were seen as the conditions for truth-telling, while constraint and need were recognized as the grounds of mendacity" (410).
13. Ibid., 238.
14. Mary Poovey. *A History of the Modern Fact: Problems of Knowledge in the Sciences of Wealth and Society*. Chicago: University of Chicago Press, 1998. "[E]arly proponents of double-entry bookkeeping," Poovey writes, "helped late sixteenth-century academics elevate the observed particular to a status that rivaled those assertions about universals that had been the cornerstone of ancient knowledge" (10).
15. Ibid., 29.
16. The merchants drew "on the rule-bound system of arithmetic," which "*seem[s]* to guarantee the accuracy of the details it recorded." My emphasis (ibid., 30).
17. Ibid., 61.
18. The "formalizing" of accounting thus "tended to privilege not just a rule-governed kind of writing but also the system of education and credentialing in which particular individuals (almost always men) were rendered obedient to such rules" (ibid., 63).
19. These hierarchies of credibility are generated out of what Laura Ephraim calls a "politics of world-building" in which "practices instantiate relations of proximity, affinity, resemblance, or repulsion among disparate human and nonhuman beings, excluding some from the assemblages that secure the power, prestige, and visibility of others." Laura Ephraim. *Who Speaks for Nature?: On the Politics of Science*. Philadelphia: University of Pennsylvania Press, 2018, 4.
20. If politics is governed by contingency and "composed of warring interests" (Poovey, *A History of the Modern Fact*, 86), commerce now appeared to be "governed by its own imminent laws" (86) and commercial decisions were made in light of "universal laws" (87). In particular, the figure of the

objective, honest merchant offered political philosophers, who were trying to elaborate a distinction between governance that benefited collective interests and that which benefited private interest, "an example of the kind of common interest that . . . a prince could recognize and represent" (89).

21. Gilmore. *Tainted Witness*, 23.
22. For example, see Martin Chulov, Chris McGreal, Lars Erikson, and Tom Kington's "Iraq War Logs: Media Reaction Around the World" (in *The Guardian*. https://www.theguardian.com/world/2010/oct/28/iraq-war-logs-media-reaction. Published October 28, 2010. Accessed September 16, 2018).
23. On the difference in how the Left/liberal public saw Snowden and Manning, see my essay, "Chelsea Manning's Integrity" (in *Jacobin*, October 3, 2016. https://www.jacobinmag.com/2016/10/chelsea-manning-edward-snowden-poitras-citizenfour-greenwald. Accessed September 21, 2017).
24. On this point, see my "Whistleblower, Traitor, Soldier, Queer?: The Truth of Chelsea Manning" (in *The Yale Review* 106(2018):1, 97–107).
25. There were some news sites that sought and published information about Snowden's private life, especially about his girlfriend. See, for example, articles on Snowden's girlfriend on the feminist pop culture website *Jezebel*, such as Erin Ryan's "Edward Snowden's Girlfriend Posts Two Mysterious New Blog Entries." (https://jezebel.com/edward-snowdens-girlfriend-posts-two-mysterious-new-blo-1691034461. Published March 12, 2015. Accessed September 12, 2018.) Yet in these pieces, as in the Stone biopic, Snowden's girlfriend's apparent fidelity to and love for Snowden served to further legitimate Snowden's credibility as a white, heterosexual man.
26. See, for example, Iris Marion Young's "Communication and the Other: Beyond Deliberative Democracy" in *Democracy and Difference*, ed. Seyla Benhabib (Princeton: Princeton University Press, 1996) and Miranda Frick's *Epistemic Injustice: Power and the Ethics of Knowing* (Cambridge: Cambridge University Press, 2007). Similarly, in *Moral Textures: Feminist Narratives in the Public Sphere* (Berkeley: University of California Press, 1998), Maria Pia Lara argues that women's narratives, articulated via

social movements, build "a bridge between the moral and the aesthetic validity spheres across the rigidly traditional gendered division between private and public" (3). For Lara, social movements can render the narratives of marginalized voices more hear-able in public.

27. Michel Foucault. *Fearless Speech*. Los Angeles: Semiotext(e), 2001, 69.

28. Michel Foucault. *The Courage of Truth*, trans. Graham Burchell. New York: Palgrave Macmillan, 2011, 2–3.

29. Foucault, *Fearless Speech*, 170.

30. Ibid., 169.

31. Ibid., 170.

32. Thus, he devotes many lectures to Plato and Socrates but barely mentions Cassandra, even when discussing Euripides' *Elektra* (where Cassandra plays a small but important role). Foucault also tends to downplay or denigrate marginalized voices when they do arise in the lectures. For example, in his discussion of Euripides's *Ion*, he acknowledges that Creusa, who has been raped by Apollo and whose truth-telling about that rape is crucial to the plot of the play (allowing her son from that rape, Ion, to gain his rightful place as an Athenian citizen), could be seen as a *parrhesiastes*, but he claims that she is a *private* truth-teller, who tells the truth only for the sake of private revenge and solace, rather than to seek public justice (which she *says* she seeks at one point in the play). On this point and Foucault's gendered conception of truth-telling more generally, see my "The Politics and Gender of Truth-Telling in Foucault's Lectures on *Parrhesia*" (in *Contemporary Political Theory* 2018. Accessed September 17, 2108. https://doi.org/10.1057/s41296-018-0224-5).

33. For example, see Nancy Luxon's "Ethics and Subjectivity" (*Political Theory* 36(2008):3, 377–402) and *The Crisis of Authority* (Cambridge: Cambridge University Press, 2013), as well as Dianna Taylor's "Resisting the Subject: A Feminist-Foucauldian Approach to Countering Sexual Violence" (*Foucault Studies* 16(2013): 88–103) and Sergei Prozorov's "Foucault's Affirmative Biopolitics: Cynic Parrhesia and the

Biopower of the Powerless" (*Political Theory*. DOI: 10.1177/0090591715609963).

34. Ella Myers. *Worldly Ethics: Democratic Politics and Care for the World*. Durham, NC: Duke University Press. On the contemporary moment as one of felt powerlessness or impasse, see Lauren Berlant. *Cruel Optimism* (Durham, NC: Duke University Press, 2011) and Ann Cvetcovich. *Depression: A Public Feeling* (Durham, NC: Duke University Press, 2012).
35. Saidiya Hartman. *Lose Your Mother: A Journey Along the Atlantic Slave Route*. New York: Farrar, Strauss, and Giroux, 2008.
36. On this point, see, for example, Naomi Klein's *The Shock Doctrine: The Rise of Disaster Capitalism* (New York: Metropolitan Books, 2007).
37. In particular, see Wendy Brown's *Undoing the Demos: Neoliberalism's Stealth Revolution* (Cambridge, MA: MIT Press, Zone Books, 2015) and Bonnie Honig's *Public Things: Democracy in Disrepair* (New York: Fordham University Press, 2017).
38. Kathi Weeks, "A Counter-Archive for the Future: Scaling Up Feminist Theory," presented at the 2017 Western Political Science Association Conference. Manuscript on file with author.
39. Further, "[w]hereas a tradition is imagined as a cumulative development through time, an archive might be read forward or backward, its sequence and composition not predetermined" (ibid., 5).
40. Ibid., 6.
41. Cooper, *Beyond Respectability*, 12.
42. Ibid.
43. Diana Taylor. *The Archive and the Repertoire: Performing Cultural Memory in the Americas*. Durham, NC: Duke University Pres, 2013, 20.
44. "The repertoire both keeps and transforms choreographies of meaning . . . Dances change over time, even though generations of dancers (and even individual dancers) swear they're always the same. But even though the embodiment changes, the meaning might very well remain the same" (Taylor, 20).

45. Ginger Thompson, "Early Struggles of Soldier Charged in Leak Case," in *New York Times*. Published August 8, 2010. http://www.nytimes.com/2010/08/09/us/09manning. html?pagewanted=all. Accessed March 14, 2013.
46. Ibid., 21.

Chapter 2

1. In *American Prophecy: Race and Redemption in American Political Culture* (Minneapolis: University of Minnesota Press, 2008), Shulman shows the richness of modern reworkings of the prophetic tradition and how that tradition—especially when used by the marginalized and oppressed—holds important resources for calling publics to awareness and action. Some of Shulman's modern prophets (especially James Baldwin) blur into outsider truth-tellers, since as Shulman says, Baldwin "announces the vicissitudes of human finitude not by way of God's righteousness in a providentially ordered universe but by way of the exemplary meaning of 'truth' of his experience as a human being and as a 'sexually dubious' black man" (132). I build on these aspects of Shulman's work, while focusing on how outsider truth-telling has immanent value: as a practice that creates *new* possibilities for living truthfully as a collective.
2. Thanks to Jill Frank for this formulation.
3. Thus, in contrast to 1930s pacifists like Bertrand Russell and Vera Brittain, who blamed government propaganda for deceiving the public, Woolf sees the public as implicated in their own deception. For example, speaking of WWI, Russell says, "Any one who will take the trouble to look up a newspaper published during the Great War will be amazed by the hot flame of insanity, melodrama, and ferocious tribal morality that leaps form the pages"; "the general public does not know what is done" (Bertrand Russell. *Which Way to Peace?* 160, 161). Similarly, Vera Brittain argues in the context of WWII that "the fog of propaganda blankets the sharp edges of truth" and that "[t]he imagination of kindly men and women

is protected from these facts [of war's violence and infliction of suffering on the innocent] because, if they were aware of what is really happening behind the drawn curtains, their decency would revolt" (Vera Brittain. "Humiliation with Honor," in *One Voice: Pacifist Writings from the Second World War*. New York: Continuum, 2005, 8, 9).

4. For example, Woolf says that men of science tried to keep women out of the professions by claiming that "nature" makes women unfit for them: "Nature it was claimed who is not only omniscient but unchanging, had made the brain of woman of the wrong shape or size" (*Three Guineas*, ed. Jane Marcus. New York: Mariner Books, 2006, 165. Hereafter cited as *TG*). Woolf's most searing critique on this score is of the university—an institution that she portrays as dependent for its financial well-being on its contributions to private industry and war. In *Three Guineas* she says, for example, "What has your college done to stimulate great manufacturers to endow it? Have you taken a leading part in the invention of the implements of war? How far have your students succeeded in business as capitalists?" (*TG*, 32).

5. Both Hartsock (in *Money, Sex, and Power: Toward a Feminist Historical Materialism*. Boston: Northeastern University Press, 1985) and Ruddick (in *Maternal Thinking: Toward a Politics of Peace*. Boston: Beacon Press, 1989) see the sexual division of labor as the crucial institution that creates distinct female and male standpoints, one of which (the male) is revealed from a feminist standpoint to be "partial and perverse." They portray women's role in the domestic realm (and in being prepared for that role) as leaving women closer to nature than men and focused on relation rather than separation. This same kind of depiction can be found in Carol Gilligan's work (*In a Different Voice*. Cambridge, MA: Harvard University Press, 1993). In contrast to identifying a woman's voice or standpoint in terms of work or role in the domestic realm, Woolf and other outsider truth-tellers characterize the private realm as largely an offshoot of public hierarchies of domination and portray the activities of that realm as equally structured by hierarchy and oppression. While Hartsock and Ruddick surely see this as well

(their main recommendations are to challenge and restructure the sexual division of labor), they see women's activities in that realm as offering a potentially emancipatory standpoint rather than being ineluctably shaped by hierarchy. In contrast, Woolf and other outsiders see truth-telling as made possible through refusing the terms of domesticity and the private realm, *as well as* refusing the terms of the public realm, thus refusing to speak as a "mother" or "wife" (categories which deplete aspects of outsider experience even if they enhance others), as well as refusing to be seen in public in the terms of dominant masculinity or its others. This not only relates to refusing the oppressive terms by which maternity and motherhood have been shaped, but also to refusing the idea that maternity and motherhood could generate truthfulness about activities, experiences, and realms that, for them, exceed those terms.

6. Michael Warner. "Public and Private," in *Publics and Counterpublics*. New York: Verso, 2005. Eve Sedgwick. *The Epistemology of the Closet*. Berkeley: University of California Press, 2008. Woolf's position differentiated her from other pacifists in the period, such as Bertrand Russell and Beverly Nichols, who also argued that public militarism is connected to the private sphere. Nichols and Russell argued that militarism is learned from the irrationality of the private realm, whereas Woolf is suggesting that it is the irrational hierarchies of public life that have shaped the private realm. Nichols, for example, argues that we must "go upstairs to the nursery" to find the origins of militarism—in the boy's toy soldiers, the stories told to him by his nurses, etc. (Beverley Nichols. *Cry Havoc!* Garden City, NY: Doubleday, 1933, 234). Bertrand Russell also says that "[m]others and nurses are the first instructors in militarism," but by this he means that children learn to use force from having it used against them as children—that is, via corporal punishment (*Which Way to Peace?* London: Jonathan Cape, 1936, 180).

7. The "private house" comes to serve patriarchal militarism by educating the subordinated (here, women) into complicity with—or sometimes active participation in—its codes. Educated for marriage, women learn in the private home to

profess and really feel support for that which men love: hierarchy and war (*TG*, 49). "It was with a view to marriage that her mind was taught. It was with a view to marriage that she tinkled on the piano, but was not allowed to join an orchestra; sketched innocent domestic scenes, but was not allowed to study from the nude; read this book, but was not allowed to read that, charmed, and talked. It was with a view to marriage that her body was educated; a maid was provided for her; that the streets were shut to her; that the fields were shut to her; that solitude was denied her—all this was enforced upon her in order that she might preserve her body intact for her husband. In short, the thought of marriage influenced what she said, what she thought, what she did" (*TG*, 48). Women also came to love war because it was their only escape from the private house; when the men were away, women finally were able to play more fully public roles. "So profound was her unconscious loathing for the education of the private house with its cruelty, its poverty, its hypocrisy, its immorality, its inanity that she would undertake any task however menial, exercise any fascination however fatal that enabled her to escape. Thus consciously she desired 'our splendid Empire'; unconsciously she desired our splendid war" (*TG*, 49). For Woolf, "the public and the private worlds are inseparably connected; . . . the tyrannies and servilities of the one are the tyrannies and servilities of the other" (*TG*, 168). As Berenice Carroll puts it, Woolf saw, "nearly half a century before the idea became widespread in the contemporary women's movement, that the 'personal is political.'" Berenice Carroll, "'To Crush Him in Our Own Country': The Political Thought of Virginia Woolf," in *Feminist Studies* 4(1978):1, 99–132, 117.

8. Thanks to Bonnie Honig for suggesting this formulation.
9. Patricia Hill Collins, "Learning from the Outsider Within: The Sociological Significance of Black Feminist Thought," in *Social Problems* 33(1986):1, 514–532, 527. Also see Collins's *Black Feminist Thought: Knowledge, Consciousness, and the Politics of Empowerment* (New York: Routledge, 2002).
10. bell hooks. *Feminist Theory: From Margin to Center*. Boston: Pluto Press, 2000, 15.

11. Audre Lorde. *Sister Outsider: Essays and Speeches*. Crossing Press, 2012, 41. Hereafter cited as *SO*.

12. Lorde says, "[f]or within living structures defined by profit, by linear power, by institutional dehumanization, our feelings were not meant to survive. Kept around as unavoidable adjuncts or pleasant pastimes, feelings were expected to kneel to thought as women were expected to kneel to men" (*SO*, 39).

13. The necessity of dialogue with others to enable confidence in one's own ability to tell the truth distinguishes outsider truth-telling from the genre of *testimonio* discussed by John Beverley (in *Testimonio: On the Politics of Truth*. Minneapolis: University of Minnesota Press, 2004). Where Beverley is interested in an "ethical and epistemological authority" (3) of the subaltern or marginalized, derived from first-hand experience and meant to interpolate (through this authority) the dominant into the narrative, I am interested in how the marginalized come to refuse the forms of authority necessary to be heard by the dominant and yet come to be able to tell the truth nonetheless.

14. Fred Moten and Stefano Harney. *The Undercommons: Fugitive Planning and Black Study*. New York: Minor Compositions, 2013. "Fugitive publics do not need to be restored. They need to be conserved, which is to say moved, hidden, restarted with the same joke, the same story, always elsewhere than where the long arm of the creditor seeks them, conserved from restoration, beyond justice, beyond law, in bad country, in bad debt. They are planned when they are least expected, planned when they don't follow the process, planned when they escape policy, evade governance, forget themselves, remember themselves, have no need of being forgiven" (64).

15. A similar impulse is at work in Patricia Hill Collins's affirmation of the experience of being an "outsider within" and in her argument to "conserve" rather than seek to overcome "the creative tension of outsider within status by encouraging and institutionalizing outsider within ways of seeing" ("Learning from the Outsider Within," 529). hooks and Gloria Anzaldua (in her account of the *mestiza*) also, like Lorde, suggest that part of the creative potential of outsider truth-telling lies in the refusal of complicity in public and private via the creation and

imagining of new spaces that exceed or break down the public/private divide. For example, Anzaldua says "The work of mestiza consciousness is to break down the subject-object duality that keeps her a prisoner and to show in the flesh and through the images in her work her duality is transcended" (in *Borderlands/La Frontera: The New Mestiza*. Aunt Lute Books, 1987, 80).

16. Lori Jo Marso. *Politics with Beauvoir: Freedom in the Encounter*. Durham, NC: Duke University Press, 2017, 201.

17. Stephen Dillon. *Fugitive Life: The Queer Politics of the Prison State*. Durham, NC: Duke University Press, 2018, 12.

18. On mere life and more life, see Bonnie Honig's "Preface" to *Emergency Politics: Paradox, Law, Democracy* (Princeton: Princeton University Press, 2009) and Lida Maxwell, "Queer/Love/Bird Extinction: Rachel Carson's *Silent Spring* as a Work of Love," in *Political Theory* 45(2017):5, 682–704.

19. For Lorde, pleasure is a resource for generating political possibility: "As a Black lesbian feminist, I have a particular feeling, knowledge, and understanding for those sisters with whom I have danced hard, played, or even fought. This deep participation has often been the forerunner for joint concerted actions not possible before" (*SO*, 59).

20. Anna Julia Cooper. *The Voice of Anna Julia Cooper: Including a Voice from the South and Other Important Essays, Letters, and Papers*. New York: Rowman and Littlefield, 2000, 51.

21. Ibid., 113.

22. Ibid., 114.

23. Brittney Cooper, *Beyond Respectability*, 5–6.

24. Anna Julia Cooper, *The Voice of Anna Julia Cooper*, my emphasis, 114.

25. By insisting on "secrecy," what Woolf means is not that individuals' *acts* must be secret, but that they must be allowed to act without publicity and without stating or publicizing their "ends" or "goals." In this sense, like Karuna Mantena's Gandhi in "Another Realism: The Politics of Gandhian Nonviolence" (*American Political Science Review* 106(2012):2, 455–470), Woolf is arguing for a practice of resistance focused on means, not ends—but Woolf's outsider practices may not amount fully to a "politics."

26. Adrienne Rich. *On Lies, Secrets, and Silence: Selected Prose 1966–1978*. New York: Norton, 1995, 187.
27. Ibid., 188.

Chapter 3

1. *Wired* released the full transcript of the chat logs in a piece entitled "Manning-Lamo Chat Logs Revealed," on July 13, 2011 (http://www.wired.com/threatlevel/2011/07/manning-lamo-logs; Accessed January 30, 2013). Throughout this essay, I will cite them parenthetically as MLCL, with page numbers that refer to the page numbers of my print-out of the chat log.
2. This is different from Foucault's *parrhesiastes*, who stakes his claim of truth on himself, on his status and reputation. See Foucault's *Fearless Speech*, ed. Joseph Pearson (Los Angeles: Semiotext(e), 2001).
3. Much of the information in this section comes from Denver Nicks's *Private: [Chelsea] Manning, Wikileaks, and the Biggest Exposure of Official Secrets in American History* (Chicago: Chicago Review Press, 2012).
4. There are, of course, separate regulations prohibiting "transsexualism" in the Army, which date to the 1960's (see, for example, Kerrigan, M. F. (2012). Transgender discrimination in the military: The new don't ask, don't tell. Psychology, Public Policy, and Law, 18(3), 500-518).I focus on Don't Ask Don't Tell in this chapter because it was Manning's primary concern.
5. Manning admitted to the leaking in her guilty plea to some of the charges leveled against her by the US Army. For this paper, I have used Alexa O'Brien's transcription of her guilty plea statement (on February 28, 2013) (http://www.alexaobrien.com/secondsight/wikileaks/bradley_manning/pfc_bradley_e_manning_providence_hearing_statement.html; Accessed February 28, 2013).
6. In her decision to reduce Manning's sentence by 112 days due to the treatment she received while in military prison, the trial judge, Denise Lind, "said Manning's confinement was 'more rigorous than necessary.' She added that the conditions 'became

excessive in relation to legitimate government interests.'"
(David Dishneau, "[Chelsea] Manning Ruling: Judge
Reduces Sentence for Army Private in WikiLeaks Case," in
The Huffington Post. Posted January 18, 2013. http://www.
huffingtonpost.com/2013/01/08/bradley-manning-ruling_n_
2432946.html. Accessed April 28, 2014.)

7. Charlie Savage, "Manning Sentenced to 35 Years for a
Pivotal Leak of U.S. Files," in *The New York Times*. Published
August 21, 2013. http://www.nytimes.com/2013/08/22/
us/manning-sentenced-for-leaking-government-secrets.
html?pagewanted=all. Accessed April 28, 2014.

8. See Manning's "A Statement on My Legal Name Change."
https://www.huffingtonpost.com/chelsea-manning/a-
statement-on-my-legal-name-change_b_5199874.html. Posted
April 23, 2014. Accessed December 20, 2018. The article notes
that Manning prefers to use "trans*" with an asterix, so as to include those who do not feel that they fit into the gender binary.

9. Yochai Benkler. "The Dangerous Logic of the [Chelsea]
Manning Case," in *The New Republic*. Http://www.newrepublic.
com/article/112554#; published March 1, 2013. Accessed
March 15, 2013.

10. Nader says, "Today, arbitrary treatment of citizens by powerful institutions has assumed a new form, no less insidious
than that which prevailed in an earlier time. The 'organization'
has emerged and spread its invisible chains. Within the structure of the organization there has taken place an erosion of
both human values and the broader value of human beings
as the possibility of dissent within the hierarchy has become
so restricted that common candour requires uncommon
courage. The large organization is lord and manor, and most
of its employees have been desensitized much as were medi-
eval peasants who never knew they were serfs. It is true that
often the immediate physical deprivations are far fewer, but the
price of this fragile shield has been the dulling of the senses
and perceptions of new perils and pressures of a far more
embracing consequence." ("The Anatomy of Whistleblowing"
in *Moral Rights in the Workplace*, ed. Gertrude Ezorsky.
Albany: SUNY Press, 1987, 89)

11. Nader, "The Anatomy of Whistleblowing," 92.

12. Ibid.

13. Most recently, Geoffrey de Lagasnerie wrote an entire book defending Snowden, Assange, and Manning as exemplifying a new form of resistant truth-telling (that interrupts contemporary forms of law and sovereignty), without mentioning Manning's gender or sexuality a single time. See his *The Art of Revolt: Snowden, Assange, Manning* (Stanford: Stanford University Press, 2017).

14. Greenwald also repeatedly stresses that public oversight of corrupt powers has been triggered by Manning's revelations (oversight also continually referred to by Manning's other supporters): for instance, that the revelation of corruption among Tunisian leaders through Cablegate was one catalyst of the Arab Spring, that revelations of US support for Iraqi practices of torture have sparked debates about torture in the United States, and that the possible criminality of the actions of US servicemen as shown in the 2007 video *Collateral Murder* triggered official investigations into the incidents. For this, Greenwald argues—like another of Manning's defenders, Chase Madar—that Manning deserves not to be treated like a traitor, but rather given a "medal." Glenn Greenwald. "[Chelsea] Manning deserves a medal," in *The Guardian*. Published December 14, 2011. Http://www.guardian.co.uk/commentisfree/2011/dec/14/bradley-manning-deserves-a-medal; Accessed March 15, 2013. For Madar's argument, see Chase Madar, "[Chelsea] Manning, American Hero," in *Le Monde Diplomatique*. Published July 19, 2011. https://mondediplo.com/openpage/bradley-manning-american-hero. Accessed September 12, 2018.

15. Nicks, *Private*, 184.

16. Manning also claims in her chats with Lamo that she was motivated by feelings of sympathy with those being harmed by US actions in Iraq and elsewhere. For instance, in her discussion with Lamo of the footage that would become the *Collateral Murder* video, Manning says that after figuring out what had happened, "it was unreal . . . i mean, i've identified bodies before . . . its rare to do, but usually its just some nobody . . . it

humanized the whole thing . . . re-sensitized me . . . i dont know . . . im just, weird i guess . . . i cant separate myself from others . . . i feel connected to everybody . . . like they were distant family . . . i . . . care?" (*MLCL*, 25–26). And in her guilty plea statement, Manning stressed that it was only after releasing the information that she felt at ease with her conscience: "Although the information had not yet been publicly released by the WLO, I felt this sense of relief by them having it. I felt I had accomplished something that allowed me to have a clear conscience based upon what I had seen and read about and knew were happening in both Iraq and Afghanistan everyday." (Manning's guilty plea statement, February 28, 2013, http://www.alexaobrien.com/secondsight/wikileaks/bradley_ manning/pfc_bradley_e_manning_providence_hearing_ statement.html. Accessed February 28, 2013.)

17. Indeed, at the same time that she was leaking documents to Wikileaks, Manning was starting to tell the truth about her struggles with gender identity to her commanding officer: "i already got myself into minor trouble, revealing my uncertainty over my gender identity . . . which is causing me to lose this job . . . and putting me in an awkward limbo" (*MLCL*, 7).

18. In this argument, I first build on Michael Warner's dual insight that the supposedly private sphere is always publicly constructed—as we can see in the gay and lesbian experience of the "closet" as private (even though it is publicly constructed by heteronormative discourse). "No one," Warner says, "ever created a closet for him- or herself. People find themselves in its oppressive conditions before they know it, willy-nilly. It is experienced by lesbians and gay men as a private, individual problem of shame and deception. But it is produced by the heteronormative assumptions of everyday talk. *It feels private. But in an important sense it is publicly constructed*" ("Public and Private," in *Publics and Counterpublics*. New York: Verso, 2005, my emphasis, 52). Warner's work builds on Eve Sedgwick's *Epistemology of the Closet* (Berkeley: University of California Press, 1990). Second, I build on Warner's argument that supposedly public, neutral, universal forms of comportment are always defined by partial (masculine, white, educated,

justificatory) forms of comportment that we tend to define as private. As Warner puts it, the traditionally liberal notion of the proper public speaker is one who possesses "[t]he ability to bracket one's embodiment and status" and thus is able to make "public use of one's reason"—a use that will be of concern to everybody, not just to those who share your identity. The problem with this classical liberal notion of the proper public speaker is that it masks the partiality of the forms of comportment that are accepted as properly public in the guise of neutrality. For Warner, the ability to bracket one's status and identity is not actually a universal human capacity—even though we often take it to be so—but "a strategy of distinction, profoundly linked to education and dominant forms of masculinity" (51).

19. J. Halberstam. *The Queer Art of Failure*. Durham, NC: Duke University Press, 2012.
20. "[Chelsea] Manning's Internet Chats with [Zinnia Jones]" in *The Guardian*. Published July 6, 2011. http://www.guardian.co.uk/world/2011/jul/07/bradley-manning-chat-logs-zach-antolak Accessed February 28, 2013.
21. Warner, "Public and Private." On the problems with supposedly "neutral" standards for judging proper public speech, also see Iris Marion Young's "Communication and the Other."
22. As Sedgwick puts it in a contrast between the practice of "coming out" as gay and Esther's famous "coming out" as a Jew to Assueres so as to save her people, Esther's "confident sense of control over other people's knowledge about her" (she knows that Assueres does *not* know) stands "in contrast to the radical uncertainty closeted gay people are likely to feel about who is in control of information about their sexual identity." Sedgwick, *Epistemology of the Closet*, 79. For Sedgwick, gay individuals lack control not only over what others "know," but also over the evidence for their own claims to be gay—or in Manning's case, gay and gender nonconforming: "In the processes of gay self-disclosure . . . in a twentieth-century context, questions of authority and evidence can be the first to arise" (ibid.). For a recent important use of Sedgwick's framework on behalf of challenging its usefulness in terms of immigration, see Demetra

Kasimis's "The Tragedy of Blood-Based Membership: Secrecy and the Politics of Immigration in Euripides' *Ion*" (in, *Political Theory* 41 (April 2013): 2, 231–256).

23. Manning tells Lamo, for example, that she hopes she "can live a less ambiguous life soon" (*MLCL*, 43) through undergoing the process of transition from male to female. She tells Lamo that she is already creating an online presence for "Breanna Manning" and that she has considered many of the practical issues of transition: "i wish it were as simple as 'hey, go transition' . . . but i need to get paperwork sorted . . . financial stuff sorted . . . legal stuff . . . and im still deployed so i have to be redeployed to the US and be outprocessed" (*MLCL*, 7).

24. On this point, see Denver Nicks's *Private*.

25. Michel Foucault. *History of Sexuality, Volume One*. New York: Vintage, 1990.

26. Foucault's own late work similarly resists any neat categorization of truth-telling as *only* reinstating expert-driven discourses of power. On this point, see especially *Fearless Speech, The Government of Self and Others*, and *The Courage of the Truth*.

27. Jacques Ranciere. *Proletarian Nights: The Workers' Dream in Nineteenth Century France*, trans. John Drury. New York: Verso, 2012, my emphasis, xi.

28. This is why Manning herself tries to have access to as much information as possible. She tells Lamo that she tries to be "aware of who's making decisions that affect me"—people like "Commanders, Politicians, Journalists, the works . . . i try to keep track . . . i have sources in the White House re: DADT and the disaster that keeps going on with that" (*MLCL*, 41). Manning's attempt to understand how decisions about Don't Ask Don't Tell (DADT) are made and implemented allowed her (she believed) to carve out a small circle of permissible behavior within a hostile terrain.

29. Jodi Dean in *Publicity's Secret* (Ithaca: Cornell University Press, 2002), similarly suggests that acts of disclosure may support rather than unsettle existing structures of power. Yet Dean also suggests that acts of disclosure are more contingent than Vismann suggests—that is, that they need not participate in,

and need not be read as participating in, the ideology of publicity that she rightly critiques. Dean argues, for example, that theorists do not have to abandon the internet as a possible site of democratic potential, but rather should "politicize" rather than "romanticize . . . the connections it [the Web] enables," "investigating and challenging the practices of linking that are employed in issue networks" (170). Read as an act of "transformative truth-telling," we could read Manning's act precisely in this way—as troubling the notion of publicness that her detractors and defenders take as an ideal and problematizing "practices of linking" that rely on gendered norms of publicness, or on the state's authority as the proper arbiter of truth.

30. Ibid., 147.

31. On the meaningfulness of solicitations to publics even when they fail to elicit the public they desire, see Lida Maxwell. *Public Trials: Burke, Zola, Arendt and the Politics of Lost Causes.* Oxford: Oxford University Press, 2014. Also see Kathi Weeks's *The Problem with Work* (Durham: Duke University Press, 2013) on the importance of making utopian demands, even if those demands are never fully met.

32. Nicks, *Private*, 183, 183–184.

33. Richard Stallman. *Free Software, Free Society: Selected Essays of Richard M. Stallman.* Boston: GNU Press, Free Software Foundation, 2002. As Stallman puts it, "[t]he term "free software" is sometimes misunderstood—it has nothing to do with price. It is about freedom." For him, "a program is free software, for you, a particular user, if: You have the freedom to run the program, for any purpose; You have the freedom to modify the program to suit your needs. (To make this freedom effective in practice, you must have access to the source code, since making changes in a program without having the source code is exceedingly difficult). You have the freedom to redistribute copies, either gratis or for a fee; You have the freedom to distribute modified versions of the program, so that the community can benefit from your improvements" (20).

34. As Stallman says, "[a]s a general rule, I don't believe that it is essential for people to have permission to modify all sorts of articles and books. For example, I don't think you or I are

obliged to give permission to modify articles like this one, which describe our actions and our views." Ibid., 30.

35. Stallman developed his theory of free information in the 1990s in opposition to the growing commodification of the internet, a commodification that—as Astra Taylor notes in *The People's Platform: Taking Back Power and Culture in the Digital Era* (New York: Picador, 2015)—reveals the limitations of the supposed democratic promise of the internet. However, as Taylor also notes, and as Fred Turner notes in *From Counterculture to Cyberculture: Stewart Brand, the Whole Earth Network, and the Rise of Digital Utopianism* (Chicago: University of Chicago Press, 2008), the vision of pure freedom that Stallman outlines never actually existed. The internet and its utopian promise were implicated in capitalist commodification and militarism from the start.

36. Dean Spade. *Normal Life: Administrative Violence, Critical Trans Politics, and the Limits of Law.* Boston: South End Press, 2011, 11.

37. Ibid., 19.

38. Jack Halberstam. *Trans: A Quick and Quirky Account of Gender Variability.* Berkeley: University of California Press, 2018, 4. Similarly, Susan Stryker, Paisley Currah, and Lisa Jean Moore prefer "trans-" to "trans" because of the "explicit relationality of 'trans-', which remains open-ended and resists premature foreclosure by attachment ot nay single suffix" ("Introduction: Trans-, trans, or transgender?" *Women's Studies Quarterly* 36(2008): 3/4, 11–22, 11).

39. For example, Halberstam says, "[w]hile new gender protocols as expressed on Facebook and in other forms of social media seem to register advancement, flexibility, and even a decentering of normative gendering, increased flexibility with regard to gender may function as part of new regulatory regimes . . . With recognition comes acceptance, with acceptance comes power, with power comes regulation" (18).

40. Reina Gossett, Eric A. Stanley, and Johanna Burton. *Trap Door: Trans Cultural Production and the Politics of Visibility,* ed. Reina Gossett, Eric A. Stanley, and Johanna Burton. Cambridge: MIT Press, 2017, xxiii.

41. Ibid., xxiii.
42. Ibid.
43. Sonali Chakravarti offers an important critique of the assumption in whistleblower defenses that outrage about disclosure will necessarily translate into reform. See her "Every Generation Fails Its Whistleblower: Ellsberg, Manning, and the Stubbornness of Democratic Debate" (presented at *Western Political Science Association Meeting*, March 2013).

Chapter 4

1. On ANONYMOUS, see Gabrielle Coleman's *Hacker, Hoaxer, Whistleblower, Spy: The Many Faces of Anonymous* (New York: Verso, 2014).
2. For a critical account of the roles of Wikileaks and Julian Assange in the 2016 election, see Tamsin Shaw's "Edward Snowden Reconsidered" (in *The New York Review of Books* https://www.nybooks.com/daily/2018/09/13/edward-snowden-reconsidered/ Published September 13, 2018. Accessed September 14, 2018).
3. Rahul Sagar. *Secrets and Leaks*. Princeton: Princeton University Press, 2016, 109–110.
4. Ibid., 5. The problem here is that "not only good men and women but also *partisans* and *zealots* take advantage of anonymity to disclose information that suits their narrow purposes" (5). Sagar argues that anonymous leaking *can* be justified if it reveals a clear moral and legal wrong (he offers Abu Ghraib and rendition as examples): a "whistleblower who reveals gross wrongdoing . . . will not be obliged to disclose her identity, as the significance of her motives will pale in comparison to the public interest in confronting a serious misuse of public authority" (137–138). Yet surely Sagar knows that even Abu Ghraib and rendition are not uncontested wrongs; in practice, these revelations were portrayed by some conservatives not as revealing a wrong, but as photos of misguided hijinks, for example, taken out of context, "fraternity

pranks" (according to Rush Limbaugh). From this perspective, most if not all anonymous leaking (including Manning's and Snowden's) would be seen as unjustified and problematic.

5. In an essay that discusses Sagar's book, David Cole similarly notes this burden that leakers put on the public: "In the end, the leaker puts both himself and society in a difficult position. By disclosing secrets, he may well burn his career, lose his liberty, and alter his life forever . . . And while we as members of the public have learned from [Snowden, Manning, and Assange] about what our government has done behind closed doors in our name, they have also taken it upon themselves to reveal hundreds of thousands of secret documents, only some of which may have been justifiably disclosed. No one elected Snowden, Manning, or Assange to act as our conscience. But if they didn't so act, who would?" David Cole, "The Three Leakers and What to Do About Them," in *New York Review of Books*. Published February 6, 2014. http://www.nybooks.com/articles/2014/02/06/three-leakers-and-what-do-about-them/ Accessed July 7, 2017.

6. Danielle Allen, "Anonymous: On Speech and Silence in the Public Sphere," in *Speech and Silence in American Law*, ed. Austin Sarat. Cambridge: Cambridge University Press, 127. While anonymous speech is "a solution when the costs of public speech have been set too high," it "also increases the costs of listening to what is said" and thus is "always a problem" (125).

7. For example, as Dana Priest and William Arkin discuss in their book, *Top Secret America*, there were actually more than 850,000 people with top secret clearance in 2010, many of whom were private contractors, not government employees. In what sense is information known by such a large number of people "secret"? One could argue that the use of "secrecy" in this context is an attempt to portray a situation of porousness and leaking as secure, rather than to actually achieve security. Dana Priest and William Arkin. *Top Secret America: The Rise of the New American Security State*. Boston: Little Brown, 2011.

8. Wendy Hui Kyong Chun. *Updating to Remain the Same: Habitual New Media*. Cambridge, MA: MIT Press, 2016, 412. Hereafter cited as *URS*, with notations of location number in the Kindle version of the book.

9. For example, Chun argues that online slut shaming "blames the user—*her* habits of leaking—for systemic vulnerabilities, glossing over the ways in which our promiscuous machines routinely work through an alleged 'leaking' that undermines the separation of the personal from the networked" (*URS*, 3651). Young women are scapegoated and targeted for a public/private blurring that is part of how the internet works.

10. "We are constantly caressed by signals that exscribe, that have everything to do with communicating, but little to do with meaning. Networks work—they allow us to communicate—by exposing YOU, by making YOU vulnerable, so that there can be a 'we,' against however inoperative, however YOUs, to begin with" (*URS*, 4066).

11. Virginia Woolf. *A Room of One's Own*. New York: Mariner, 2005, my emphasis, 50–51.

12. Ibid., 52.

13. Ibid., 115.

14. Woolf, "Anon.," in "'Anon' and 'The Reader': Virginia Woolf's Last Essays," ed. Brenda Silver. *Twentieth Century Literature* 25(1979):3/4, 380-393, 383.

15. As Saidiya Hartman argues in "Venus in Two Acts," the archive itself is constituted through violence that enshrines some voices in written memory, and leaves others (notably, those enslaved in the United States) inaudible, unrecorded. In *Small Axe: A Caribbean Journal of Criticism* 12(2008):2: 1–14.

16. James E. Bristol, Amiya Chakravarty, A. Burns Chalmers, William B. Edgerton, Harrop A. Freeman, Robert Gilmore, Cecil E. Hinshaw, Milton Mayar, A.J. Muste, Clarence E. Pickett, Robert Pickus, Norman J. Whitney, and Bayard Rustin, [his name was restored to the list of authors in 2010]. "Speak Truth to Power," prepared for the American Friends Service Committee, 1955. https://www.afsc.org/sites/afsc.civicactions.net/files/documents/Speak_Truth_to_Power.pdf. Accessed on August 17, 2017. Hereafter cited as *STP* in the text.

17. Bayard Rustin. *I Must Resist: Bayard Rustin's Life in Letters*. San Francisco: City Lights Publishers, 2012, 161. Hereafter cited as *IMR*.

18. In John D'Emilio's biography of Rustin (*Lost Prophet: The Life and Times of Bayard Rustin*. New York: Free Press, 2003), as in Rustin's letters, this is the dominant depiction of his homosexuality by his pacifist mentor, A. J. Muste, as well as by other pacifist colleagues, as I go on to discuss in the text.

19. Saying that he is writing out of "love" (*IMR*, 75), Muste says that "there are *some limits* to self-indulgence" (76): "Don't you see that with your undiscipline, deceit practiced on your dearest comrades, superficiality, jumping about, arrogance, you are—in one sense—running away from yourself and—in another—destroying yourself?" (76). Muste says that Rustin can find "true love" if he gives up "what amounts to a death wish almost for insecurity, for attachment which never is attachment," but rather "a surface tickling of yourself and an exploitation of others" (77).

20. Indeed, the *Speak Truth to Power* pamphlet was an extended critique of rising US militarism that relies on the integrity of its authors (Quaker truth-tellers) to vindicate its credibility. As the authors write: "[i]f ever truth reaches power, if ever it speaks to the individual citizen, it will not be the argument that convinces. Rather it will be *his own inner sense of integrity* that impels him to say, 'Here I stand. Regardless of relevance or consequence, I can do no other'" (my emphasis, *STP*, 68). The integrity of the authors, evident in their self-sacrifice, aims in turn to stir the integrity of their audience; Rustin's decision to remove himself could be read as recognition that he currently *lacks* that integrity and must work more deeply on himself to achieve it. The authors push the point further in the closing of the pamphlet, noting that their practice of peace, their truth-telling, "means flying in the face of 'hard facts.' It is a course of action which 'common sense' at once refuses" (68).

21. D'Emilio, *Lost Prophet*, 372, chaps. 11, 9.

22. For example, D'Emilio attributes the Adam Clayton Powell and King episode to "hidden homophobia" (ibid., 372), but D'Emilio also frequently ascribes Rustin's failure to move to the

forefront of the civil rights movement to a personal failure on Rustin's part to adequately temper his sexuality. For instance, D'Emilio faults Rustin for not remaining celibate in prison and thus, for leaving himself open to charges from the prison administration that disrupted his anti-segregation campaign. D'Emilio says: "Spending long days alone in a cell, Rustin had plenty of time to reflect on his situation. As a leader in a movement grounded in moral rectitude, he had demonstrated *an alarming lapse of integrity and judgment*. In choosing quick physical pleasure, he had traded his hope of bearing witness against injustice for the withering censure of a system—and a society—that had little tolerance for his brand of sexual desire. And he had compounded one mistake with another when he lied to protect himself from disgrace" (my emphasis, 101).

23. Ibid., 68.
24. Ibid., 71.
25. Ibid., 219.
26. Writing to Davis Platt in April of 1945, Rustin says that "[e]motionally, I am at present strongly attached to Marie [his code word for Platt in his letters]; intellectually, I know that every effort must be made to find a different solution, for my vocation, which is my life, is at stake" (*IMR*, 70).
27. Ibid., 114.
28. Ibid., 191.
29. Although see Alex Livingston's "Fidelity to Truth" on why this alignment of Gandhi with the western tradition is problematic.
30. In this respect, Quaker discourse is continuous with Gandhi's attempt to claim that some forms of self-sacrifice are worth more than others. Gandhi distinguishes firmly, for example, between "passive resistance" and *satyagraha* because, in Dennis Dalton's words, passive resistance "allowed for 'internal violence,' the harboring of enmity and anger among resisters even when they commit no violence" (Dennis Dalton. *Mahatma Gandhi: Nonviolent Power in Action*. New York: Columbia University Press, 2012, 16). The problem here is that if resisters do not have the right motives—if they do not rule themselves, in Gandhi's language—any victory they achieve will be undermined by the violence and

unruliness of their souls; their victory will not end a cycle of violence, but simply allow for a shift in *who* exercises force and violence. In Alex Livingston's words, Gandhi's "politics of non-violence . . . makes self-sacrifice the fullest expression of self-rule" ("Fidelity to Truth," 4). Banu Bargu notes a similar dynamic at work in her study of Turkish hunger strikers. In his *Starve and Immolate* (New York: Columbia University Press, 2014), Bargu notes that party elites did not accept all rationales for self-sacrifice. Party elites were concerned in part with whether "the militant was capable of carrying out a fast unto death," but also whether they were "deserving of the lofty honor of being a martyr." In particular, "if a militant wanted to participate primarily for self-fulfilling reasons, such as seeking personal glory, she would most surely be rejected by the party organization . . . Militants who volunteered themselves had to be motivated by a sound conception of the 'objective' responsibility of a revolutionary, which was supposed to be altogether different from an eagerness to die" (246).

31. Kevin Quashie. *The Sovereignty of Quiet*. New Brunswick, NJ: 2012, 21.

32. Similarly, Tara Bynum reads Phyllis Wheatley's letters with her friend Obur Tanner: "She also leaves us with correspondence that demands a reconsideration of the archive, what we expect to find inside it, and what terms we use to bear witness to the realities of black women—in particular, those who look for each other in the Word of God and on the words of the page" ("Phyllis Wheatley on Friendship," in *Legacy* 31(2014):1, 42–51).

33. Quashie, *The Sovereignty of Quiet*, p. 34.

34. Ibid.

35. In contrast, Quashie argues that a concept of quiet reveals the "inexpressible expressiveness" of an interior constituted by a "vastness and wildness [that] often escape definitive characterization." Ibid., 22, 21.

36. Ibid., 21. Quashie's concept of quiet thus works in tandem with Mahmood's *The Politics of Piety* (Princeton: Princeton University Press, 2011) to critique the western idea that meaning is exhausted in categories of domination/oppression and resistance/liberation.

37. Patchen Markell, "The Rule of the People: Arendt, Arche, and Democracy," in *American Political Science Review* 100(2006):1, 1–14.

Chapter 5

1. Paul Virilio. *War and Cinema*. London: Verso, 1984.
2. W. J. T. Mitchell. *Cloning Terror: The War of Images, 9/11 to the Present*. Chicago: University of Chicago Press, 2011, 122.
3. On the problems with dominant liberal/left framings of the Abu Ghraib photos as problematic because of their sexual humiliation of Arab men, see Jasbir Puar's *Terrorist Assemblages* (Durham, NC: Duke University Press, 2007).
4. Sontag says that Woolf, "[i]nvoking this hypothetical shared experience ('we are seeing with you the same dead bodies, the same ruined houses'), . . . professes to believe that the shock of such pictures cannot fail to unite people of good will" (*Regarding the Pain of Others*. New York: Farrar, Strauss, and Giroux, 2003, 6). "It is this 'we' that Woolf challenges at the start of her book: she refuses to allow her interlocutor to take a 'we' for granted. But into this 'we,' after the pages devoted to the feminist point, she then subsides" (7).
5. Ibid., 26.
6. Ibid., 13.
7. Ibid., 10.
8. Indeed, she notes that "[i]n the current political mood, the friendliest to the military in decades, the pictures of wretched hollow-eyed GIs that once seemed subversive of militarism and imperialism may seem inspirational. Their revised subject: ordinary American young men doing their unpleasant, ennobling duty" (ibid., 38).
9. Ibid., 115.
10. Ibid., 117. They are an invitation, Sontag says, "to pay attention, to reflect, to learn, to examine the rationalizations for mass suffering offered by established powers" (117).

11. Butler says, "[j]ust as the 'matter' of bodies cannot appear without a shaping and animating form, neither can the 'matter' of war appear without a conditioning and facilitating form or frame . . . So there is no way to separate, under present historical conditions, the material reality of war from those representational regimes through which it operates and which rationalize its own operation" (*Frames of War.* New York: Verso, 2016, 29).

12. If "popular assent to war is cultivated and maintained" by "war waging act[ing] upon the senses so that war is thought to be an inevitability, something good, or even a source of moral satisfaction" (ix), then the capacity of photographs to reveal their own frame offers a site of resistance to the affective and sensory conditions that make war possible. She says, "this very reproducibility entails a constant breaking from context, a constant delimitation of new context, which means that the 'frame' does not quite contain what it conveys, but breaks apart every time it seeks to give definitive organization to its content. In other words, the frame does not hold anything together in one place, but itself becomes a kind of perpetual breakage, subject to a temporal logic by which it moves form place to place. As the frame constantly breaks from its context, this self-breaking becomes part of the very definition" (ibid.,10).

13. Ibid., 11.

14. Ibid., 98.

15. For Butler, this grievability is not just affective but also demands a certain "acknowledgment," which is "also a potential judgment" that "requires that we conceive of grievability as the precondition of life, one that is discovered retrospectively through the temporality instituted by the photograph itself" (ibid.).

16. See, for example, Maggie Humm's "Memory, Photography, and Modernism: The 'Dead Bodies and Ruined Houses' of Virginia Woolf's *Three Guineas*," in *Signs* 28(2003):645–663; and Jane Marcus's "Introduction" to *Three Guineas*.

17. Susan Sontag, "Regarding the Torture of Others," in *The New York Times*. Published May 23, 2004. http://www.nytimes.

com/2004/05/23/magazine/regarding-the-torture-of-others. html. Accessed April 7, 2017.

18. On this point, see Hermione Lee's *Virginia Woolf* (New York: Vintage, 1999).

19. David Finkel. *The Good Soldiers*. New York: Farrar, Straus, and Giroux, 2009.

20. Both versions are available here: https://collateralmurder. wikileaks.org. Accessed April 7, 2017.

21. Elisabeth Bumiller, "Video Shows U.S. Killing of Reuters Employees," in *The New York Times*. Published April 5, 2010. Accessed April 6, 2017. http://www.nytimes.com/2010/04/06/ world/middleeast/06baghdad.html.

22. See, for example, Nathan Hodge's "U.S. Military Releases Redacted Records on 2007 Apache Attack, Questions Linger," in *Wired*, Posted April 7, 2010. https://www.wired. com/2010/04/military-releases-report-on-2007-apache- attack-and-questions-linger. Accessed April 6, 2017. Also, Raffi Katchadourian's "The Wikileaks Video and the Rules of Engagement," in *The New Yorker*. Published April 5, 2010. http://www.newyorker.com/news/news-desk/the-wikileaks- video-and-the-rules-of-engagement. Accessed April 6, 2010.

23. Chamayou. *A Theory of the Drone*, trans. Janet Lloyd. New York: The New Press, 2015, 12.

24. In *Hunting Girls* (New York: Columbia University Press, 2016), Kelly Oliver suggests that a certain form of masculinity in our contemporary moment may also be structured by the attempt to avoid the risk of vulnerability to female response and rejec- tion: namely, the fetishization of unconscious girls and the use of drugs and alcohol to incapacitate women rather than risk re- jection to male advances. As she puts it at one point, "claiming to sexually assault and rape, and imagining unconscious girls as 'dead girls,' are not only acceptable behaviors among young men, but also perhaps prerequisites to establish certain types of macho masculinity" (72). Rather than risk rejection, college boys simply knock their prey out; masculinity becomes about avoiding risk, rather than encountering it. "Certainly, 'sex' with inanimate girls is not about intimacy, and perhaps not even pleasure, but control" (93). Indeed, whereas risk-taking used

to be gendered masculine, Oliver's account implies that it is now gendered feminine—and that risk-taking now appears as damaging vulnerability, as a way of opening oneself up to being beaten, battered, and killed, rather than as an occasion for heroism.

25. http://www.commondreams.org/views/2010/04/16/open-letter-reconciliation-and-responsibility-iraqi-people. April 16, 2010. Accessed April 7, 2017.

26. *Incident in New Baghdad*. Dir. James Spione. Morninglight Films, 2012.

27. This is all recounted in *Incident in New Baghdad*.

28. Ibid.

29. Ibid.

30. While Ryan Searles, a medic, agrees that overall events transpired as McCord describes, he claims that it was he and not McCord who took both children to the Bradley. McCord saw the children and lifted the boy out of the van, but did not actually carry them to the Bradley, on Searles's account. As David Montgomery, a *Washington Post* reporter notes, there is no real way to adjudicate this dispute ("What Happened in Iraq," in *The Washington Post*. Published February 21, 2012. https://www.washingtonpost.com/lifestyle/style/what-happened-in-iraq/2012/02/17/gIQA08oCSR_story.html?noredirect=on&utm_term=.516e361249ff. Accessed August 23, 2018). There is no way to tell from the video footage which soldier is carrying the children; both McCord and Searles have been consistent in their accounts; and both men "sound sincere and certain" (ibid). As an epistemological question of true knowledge, then, there is no way to tell who the real factual truth-teller is here; indeed, McCord and Searles may not actually know. Yet I have been theorizing a practice of truth-telling here that is less about assessing epistemological validity and more about developing the capacity to speak truths about the experiences of the marginalized that are disavowed or declared unbelievable by the dominant society, and about creating outsider connections that enable that capacity *and* give it at least a ghostly reality. While McCord is a white, straight man, his willingness to be called into truth-telling by the release of the *Collateral Murder*

footage, his making of connections with other soldiers with un-popular anti-war beliefs, and his willingness to speak about the truth of his vulnerability and broken-ness in war to a society that saw that truth as in-credible, marks him as having been pulled into the margins of outsider truth-telling: revealing the reality of the Iraq war for soldiers and Iraqis, beyond the brief moment memorialized in *Collateral Murder*.

31. Kim Zetter, "US Soldier on 2007 Apache Attack: What I Saw," April 20, 2010. https://www.wired.com/2010/04/2007-iraq-apache-attack-as-seen-from-the-ground/. Accessed April 7, 2017.

Chapter 6

1. Among many possible examples, see McIntyre's *Post-Truth*, Casey Williams's "Has Trump Stolen Philosophy's Critical Tools?" (in *The New York Times*, Published April 17, 2017. https://www.nytimes.com/2017/04/17/opinion/has-trump-stolen-philosophys-critical-tools.html?mcubz=1. Accessed 9/21/2017) and Conor Lynch's "Trump's War on Environment and Science are Rooted in his Post-Truth Politics—and Maybe in Postmodern Philosophy" (in *Salon*, April 1, 2017. http://www.salon.com/2017/04/01/trumps-war-on-environment-and-science-are-rooted-in-his-post-truth-politics-and-maybe-in-postmodern-philosophy/. Accessed 9/21/2017).

2. In *The Death of Truth*, Michiko Kakutani writes, for example, "relativism has been ascendant since the culture wars began in the 1960s. Back then, it was embraced by the New Left, eager to expose the biases of Western, bourgeois, male-dominated thinking; and by academics promoting the gospel of post-modernism, which argued that there are no universal truths, only smaller personal truths—perceptions shaped by the cultural and social forces of one's day. Since then, relativistic arguments have been hijacked by the populist Right, including creationists and climate change deniers who insist that their views be taught alongside 'science-based' theories" (18).

3. Gilmore, *Tainted Witness.*
4. On Black Lives Matter, see Yahmatta-Taylor's *From Black Lives Matter to Black Liberation.*
5. For example, in a September 16, 2014 piece on ISIS ("How to Make ISIS Fall on Its Own Sword," https://www.theguardian.com/commentisfree/2014/sep/16/chelsea-manning-isis-strategy. Accessed September 21, 2017), she says that "when the west fights fire with fire, we feed into a cycle of outrage, recruitment, organizing and even more fighting that goes back decades. This is exactly what happened in Iraq during the height of a civil war in 2006–2007, and it can only be expected to occur again." Similarly, she argues in a March 9, 2015 piece, "The CIA's Torturers and the Leaders Who Approved Their Actions Must Face the Law" (https://www.theguardian.com/commentisfree/2015/mar/09/cia-torture-leaders-aprroved-must-face-the-law. Accessed September 21, 2017), that the use of force breeds more hatred and violence, not security: torture of prisoners by CIA officers "have gravely damaged the credibility of the US intelligence community for decades to come" and "they also may have prevented the US from being able to quickly and effectively prosecute the very terrorists who these officers sough to help fight against. This is evident by the unending stalemate in the military commissions taking place at Guantanamo Bay, Cuba." To let the torturers go unpunished would "send an awful message to the world: it is wrong to torture and mistreat people, except when those doing it have the supposed blessing of the law and with the permission of high-ranking supervisors and politicians."
6. Chelsea Manning. "We Must Not Let the Orlando Night Club Terror Further Strangle Our Civil Liberties," in *The Guardian.* Published June 13, 2016. https://www.theguardian.com/commentisfree/2016/jun/13/chelsea-manning-civil-liberties-orlando-terrorism. Accessed September 16, 2018.
7. Chelsea Manning, "On the Intersection of the Military and Prison Industrial Complex," in *Captive Genders: Trans Embodiment and the Prison Industrial Complex*, ed. Eric Stanley and Nat Smith. Oakland: AK Press, 2011, 2015. "[T]he military-industrial complex," Manning says, "determine[s]

how individuals and groups in societies get labeled as enemies or terrorists. This is also how certain behaviors and actions can become associated with terrorism . . . and determined as threats to national security" (186). Similarly, the "prison-industrial complex," she says, "determine[s] how individuals and groups in society are labeled as criminal, how certain behaviors and actions in society become associated with criminals and are classified as crimes liable to punishment by the law" (186).

8. Ibid., 187
9. Ibid., 188.
10. Ibid.
11. Building on her view of the military and prisons as creating greater insecurity for marginalized groups, Manning develops a critical view of queer and trans politics that focus on state-based recognition (such as marriage) and security (such as hate crime legislation), arguing that they generate greater surveillance of, and risk for, the most vulnerable: trans women, queers of color, etc. For example, in "Same-Sex Marriage Isn't Equality for All LGBT People. Our Movement Can't End" (in *The Guardian*. Published June 26, 2015. https://www. theguardian.com/commentisfree/2015/jun/26/same-sex-marriage-equality-all-lgbt-people-our-movement-chelsea-manning. Accessed September 21, 2017), Manning worries that the achievement of "full marriage equality" might produce a problematic political complacency in the queer community. Challenging that complacency in another piece ("I Am a Transgender Woman and the Government is Denying My Civil Rights," in *The Guardian*. Published December 8, 2014. https://www.theguardian.com/commentisfree/2014/dec/08/chelsea-manning-transgender-rights. Accessed September 21, 2017), and echoing Dean Spade's critique of dominant LGBT politics' focus on marriage rights and hate crimes legislation (that aligns them with law enforcement), Manning argues that there are crucial battles to be fought on behalf of trans equality. Manning says that the main problems for trans people lie in everyday life issues, like getting a drivers' license, discrimination in employment and housing, and receiving adequate and sensitive medical treatment. Manning notes that "the problem

is not just inclusion or equal opportunities in institutions like government identification systems or voting—because such systems are inherently, if indirectly, biased to favor high income, straight, white cisgender people. How can trans people change a system to which we don't even have access?"

12. Manning, "We Must Not Let the Orlando Night Club Terror Further Strangle Our Civil Liberties."
13. In "Facing my Fear: Being in Public as a Woman for the Very First Time" (in *The Guardian*. Published August 19, 2016. https://www.theguardian.com/commentisfree/2016/aug/19/ chelsea-manning-dont-ask-dont-tell-facing-my-fear-column. Accessed September 21, 2017)
14. Manning, "On the Intersection of the Military and Prison Industrial Complex," 198.
15. Chelsea Manning, "Prison Keeps Us Isolated," in *The Guardian*, https://www.theguardian.com/commentisfree/2016/feb/ 08/chelsea-manning-prison-keeps-us-isolated-sisterhood-transgender-friendship. Published February 8, 2016. Accessed September 21, 2017.
16. "To Those Who Kept Me Alive All These Years: Thank You," in The Guardian. Published February 13, 2017. https://www. theguardian.com/commentisfree/2017/feb/13/chelsea-manning-prison-sentence-commutation. Accessed September 21, 2017.
17. Manning, for example, attended an alt-right party that she intended to "crash," but was perceived by those on the Left as offering support and visibility. (Kyle Swenson, "Chelsea Manning Showed Up at a Far-Right, Pro-Trump bash, Infuriating the Far Left," in *The Washington Post*. Published January 23, 2018. https://www.washingtonpost.com/news/ morning-mix/wp/2018/01/23/chelsea-manning-showed-up-at-a-far-right-pro-trump-bash-infuriating-the-far-left/?utm_ term=.a7084ff3de86. Accessed September 16, 2018.)

ACKNOWLEDGMENTS

This book began in 2011 with questions about why Chelsea Manning's defenders did not (at the time) talk about her gender identity. These questions pushed me in turn to engage big questions about truth, gender, and politics, and then I came back again to Chelsea Manning. I have been lucky to have had a wide variety of interlocutors, readers, and audiences along the way.

Of course, *Insurgent Truth* would not exist if it were not for Chelsea Manning. I have never met her, but her courageous actions and words inspired this book. I am deeply in her debt.

An early set of discussions with Sonali Chakravarti about whistleblowing and an opportunity to write a paper for a Western Political Science Association panel on truth and politics were the origins of this book. Thanks to Sonali for those conversations and for her support and ongoing engagement throughout this project.

I wrote much of the original draft of this manuscript while a Mellon Midcareer Fellow at the Yale Whitney Humanities Center in 2016–2017. I am very grateful for the resources provided by the Center and the Mellon Foundation, which gave me a full year of free time to write in the context of a vibrant intellectual community. I am especially grateful to the director of the Whitney, Gary Tomlinson, as well as to Norma Thompson, for their support of the project, as well as for the delicious weekly lunches. The project was also improved by feedback I received from two presentations at Yale—one at the Whitney and one in the Political Theory Workshop, where Alyssa Battistoni gave me very helpful comments.

Trinity College was a wonderful place to begin this project. My former colleagues in the Political Science Department offered intellectual engagement and support. Thanks especially to Tony Messina and Stefanie Chambers, who (as chairs of the department) showed unfailing support for me in unique circumstances. Boston University has been a great place to finish this project, and I am grateful to my new colleagues in Political Science and Women's, Gender, and Sexuality Studies for their interest in and support of this project, especially Neta Crawford, Cati Connell, Susanne Sreedhar, David Mayers, Jim Schmidt, Gina Sapiro, Judy Swanson, and Spencer Piston.

I am grateful to various audiences who asked great questions about different parts of the project. I presented my essay on Foucault, gender, and *parrhesia* in front of a few different audiences, which helped me nail down my overall concerns about gender and truth-telling—even if the actual essay on Foucault did not end up being part of the book. Thanks to all of these audiences, especially to Yves Winter (who gave discussant comments on a WPSA panel) and Ayten Gündoğdu (who invited me to present the paper at the Columbia Seminar for Social and Political Thought) for their incisive comments. Questions and conversations with a Georgetown University audience in the spring of 2018 helped me to think through Bayard Rustin's role in the book. Thanks especially to Nolan Bennett, Corey Fields, and Josh Cherniss for the terrific thoughts and discussion. An early presentation on Chelsea Manning at the University of Minnesota Political Theory Colloquium helped me frame the project. Thanks especially to Nancy Luxon, Joan Tronto, David Temin, Elena Gambino, and Chase Hobbes-Morgan for their thoughts and questions.

I taught several versions of a course on "Truth, Lies, and Politics" at Trinity College, and I thank all of the students who were in those courses for engaging in these questions with me, especially Silvia Fedi and Emily Popov, whose questions and thoughts helped shape my own.

An earlier version of Chapter 3 appeared in *Theory and Event* as "Truth in Public: Chelsea Manning, Gender Identity, and the Politics of Truth-Telling" (18[2015]:1). I thank the journal for permission to use portions of that article here.

I am grateful to the many people who have offered thoughts, read chapters, and engaged in conversations with me over the years about this project, especially Ella Myers, Demetra Kasimis, Jill Locke, Elizabeth Wingrove, Lori Marso, Karuna Mantena, Alex Livingston, Lawrie Balfour, Jason Frank, Alison McQueen, Vicki Hsueh, Karen Zivi, Kevin McMahon, Lisa Disch, Chris Hager, Diego Rossello, Libby Anker, Ayten Gündoğdu, Yves Winter, Jane Bennett, Nancy Luxon, Shane Ewegen, Jeremy Menchik, Cati Connell, Nolan Bennett, Isaac Kamola, Rob Corber, Alyssa Battistoni, and Nina Hagel. Early discussant comments from Linda Zerilli about my paper on Chelsea Manning were—as usual—illuminating and important for my thinking. A conversation with Jill Frank about the book happened at just

the right time, and helped me sharpen my conceptualization of outsider truth-telling. Astra Taylor gave me insightful
comments that helped me sharpen the first few chapters of
the book. Angela Chnapko has been talking with me about
this book since its beginnings, and I am grateful for her edi-
torial voice and support. Darlene Millman has helped me to
become a more authentic thinker and writer.

Some people deserve special thanks. Thanks to Sara
Kippur for reading various drafts of papers that made it into
this book, for having many conversations with me about it,
and for just generally being a supportive friend who assured
me that there was something to this project and encouraged
me to pursue it. And thanks to Sara and Josh Lambert for
helping me realize that I did not have to make this book
about the whole history of political thought! Thanks also to
Sara, Josh, Noemi, and Asher, for so generously sharing their
home with me in West Hartford, which I continue to regard
as my home away from home.

Lena Zuckerwise and Laura Grattan heroically read the
first full draft of this manuscript and gave me invigorating,
helpful comments that made the whole thing better. Lori
Marso and David Gutterman read the entire manuscript in
a later form and gave me terrific comments, which made the
book better, sharper, and deeper.

It has been a real perk of this project that it brought me
into contact with Shalini Satkunanandan, and our resulting
friendship and academic engagement has benefited the book,
and me. Shalini has read various drafts and parts of this
manuscript, challenged me in ways big and small, and our
conversations have left their imprint all over this book. Laura
Ephraim has been my cherished interlocutor and friend now
for almost fifteen years. Her work on truth and science, and

our conversations about Manning and truth, were part of the origins of this project, and I feel so lucky that I continue to have the benefit of her insights on my work and of her friendship. Her meticulous read of the penultimate draft was particularly helpful. If there are any remaining problems with the book, I am sure that it is due to my failure to adopt all of her smart suggestions.

Bonnie Honig has been talking with me about this project since it began. Our conversations (and email exchanges) are always illuminating for me, and talking with her about theory is so invigorating! Thanks to Bonnie for sharing her keen insight, friendship, and unsettling brilliance with me. Thanks also to Bonnie for helping me become unstuck in the very final stages of writing.

While I have been writing about truth-telling in this book, I have been surrounded by three small truth-tellers in my house, who have made my life more vibrant and cacophonous—and always interesting! Louisa's smart questions about politics, and her unflinching sense of justice, have found their way into the pages of this book. Ezra's imagination has inspired my own, and his humor helps me to never take myself too seriously. Arlo's generosity to others has served as an intellectual example for me, as has his instinct for great storytelling. Thanks also to my parents, Carol Maxwell and Phil Maxwell, for their ongoing support and love, and to the broader Maxwell, Cunha, and Brown-Saracino families. Thanks especially to Pam Brown for her amazing help with taking care of our children over these past couple of years; without that help, none of this would be.

I am grateful to friends who provided all kinds of support and love while I was writing this book, especially Lauren Graber, Ruth Chaffee, Katherine Biers, Katherine Lieber, Kate

Leary, Chris AhnAllen, Julie AhnAllen, Jeremy Menchik, and Amber Wong. While I was in the middle of writing this book, I started, with a friend, a short-lived neighborhood political group. While I am apparently not terrifically skilled in political organizing, I thank everyone who was involved, and especially Gwen, Cara, and Mneesha. That experience informed this book in more ways than one, and reminded me that there is so much more beyond the book.

This book is dedicated to Japonica Brown-Saracino, an unfailing truth-teller, who has supported me in so many ways as I wrote this book. For now more than fifteen years, Japonica has been an inspiring intellectual interlocutor, my best friend, and the person I most want to hang out with. It is impossible to capture in words how grateful I am for her love, support, and intellectual engagement through years of having children, navigating our "two body problem," buying and selling houses, writing books, tending gardens, traveling for talks and conferences, dealing with exploding hot water heaters, mourning the passing of beloved grandparents, staying up all night with sick children, and all of the other material, affective, intellectual, and practical matters that compose a shared life. Out of that life, and the love, energy, and richness with which Japonica has invested it, comes this book. She deserves this dedication and so much more.

INDEX